Cheers to the Diaper Y   a healthy
heaping of God's grac   ide for
thriving in this crazy, beautiful journey of motherhood. This book
needs to be on every momma's bookshelf smack dab between their
Bible and *What to Expect When You're Expecting.*

> —BETSY COOPER, *head of Briarwood Presbyterian Church's*
> *Mother's Day Out program, mother to two,*
> *and grandmother to nine*

Cheers to the Diaper Years is like a refreshing gulp of sweet tea and
a lingering hug for weary mamas everywhere. This delightful read
is filled to the brim with biblical wisdom and humorous stories
that "perfect mom" wannabes can relate to. Thank you, Erin, for
changing my perspective on parenting from "I've got to mom now"
drudgery to "I get to mom now" delight.

> —TRACY STEEL, *fellow mama of two "spirited" kiddos,*
> *author, speaker, and writer; tracymsteel.com*

The infant and preschool years of parenting are physically and
emotionally exhausting. Erin Hollis quickly earns readers' trust with
humorous, relatable stories of her own surprises, disappointments,
and failures along the journey of motherhood. But she does not join
us there to wallow in a pity party! Erin makes you feel that you are
chatting with a friend over coffee as she shares how each of these
moments is really an opportunity to better understand God's grace.
Her timely truths remind moms of the importance of perspective,
community, self-forgiveness, and unconditional love—qualities that
can only be found through a growing relationship with Jesus.

> —BROOKE GIBSON, *minister to preschoolers,*
> *Dawson Family of Faith; speaker and writer*
> *for Group Publishing, Loveland, Colorado*

Delightful, encouraging, and perfectly lovely! Erin Brown Hollis's *Cheers
to the Diaper Years* brings with it a fresh glimpse of motherhood. Her
wit and honesty address the not-so-glamorous side of mommy life,
celebrating it with a cup of truth and humor. The Southern charm

laced throughout is contagious—mothers in all seasons of life will find themselves saying, "Cheers to the diaper years!"

—LAUREN H. BRANDENBURG, *author of*
The Books of the Gardener, homeschool advocate,
and mother to Kensi and Jack; www.LaurenHBrandenburg.com

Laugh-out-loud, honest, and utterly relatable. Erin Hollis has perfectly described in *Cheers to the Diaper Years* what all moms go through on a daily basis and how striving for perfection in a "perfect Instagram world" is not only unattainable but not what God calls us to.

—REAGAN CROYLE PHILLIPS, *Big Oak Ranch Childcare Director*

I so appreciate how Erin uses Scripture to encourage and enlighten us in our motherhood journey. It is beautiful to see God's design for motherhood as explained throughout His Word! Erin reminds moms that we are not perfect (and shouldn't expect perfection!), sometimes we need naps (amen!), and all of the hard, exhausting moments are worth it. Finding a mom tribe is necessary for sanity, and this book goes through how to find the fellow moms who get you and will walk alongside you to build you up when you are losing your sanity. So, log out of all your social media accounts (that are probably making you feel like a bad mom anyway), and read this book. It will have you laughing in agreement and give you encouragement to face each day with a renewed hope.

—JULIE SASSE, *co-owner and co-founder*
of Birmingham Moms Blog, and mother of two

With three kids under five and a faith not much older, I wish I'd had a friend like Erin to tell me I'm not alone, I'm not crazy, and bad mom days don't make me a bad mom. Erin's southern wit and charm ooze the Christ-centered wisdom every mom in the trenches of parenting needs for thriving in these challenging, beautiful years. Thriving is surviving with benefits, and these words will point you to the One who can and will provide them.

—NIKI HARDY, *author, speaker, thriver,*
and English breakfast tea drinker; www.nikihardy.com

CHEERS TO THE DIAPER YEARS

10 Truths for Thriving While Barely Surviving

Erin Brown Hollis

BroadStreet
PUBLISHING

BroadStreet Publishing® Group, LLC

Savage, Minnesota, USA

BroadStreetPublishing.com

Cheers to the Diaper Years: 10 Truths for Thriving While Barely Surviving

Copyright © 2018 Erin Brown Hollis

978-1-4245-5734-9 (softcover)

978-1-4245-5735-6 (e-book)

Stock or custom editions of BroadStreet Publishing titles may be purchased in bulk for educational, business, ministry, fundraising, or sales promotional use. For information, please email info@broadstreetpublishing.com.

Literary agent, Julie Gwinn, from The Seymour Agency

Cover design by Chris Garborg at garborgdesign.com

Interior design and typesetting by Katherine Lloyd at theDESKonline.com

Printed in the United States of America

18 19 20 21 22 5 4 3 2 1

Bellalise and Annalise,

*You make every day of mommy life worth celebrating.
I love you both to God and back a million bajillion times.*

CONTENTS

PART I
Mommyhood: You Have Been Chosen
TRUTH #1 – You Were Selected by God
to Be Momma to Your Babies

PART II
You Do You—Free Yourself from the Chains of Keeping Up
and Embrace the New (Non-Perfect) Mom Inside
TRUTH #2 – You Are More Than Enough in Christ

PART III
You Are Not Alone
TRUTH #3 – You Always Have Support in Christ
and In Your Tribe (Even at 2:00 a.m.)

PART IV
Conquering the Cray-Cray and
Overcoming the Chaos of #MomLife
TRUTH #4 – You Can Find Joy Even in the Craziness

PART V
Mamarazzis, Pinterest Princesses,
and MomBots, Oh My!
TRUTH #5 – You Are Never Going to Be Perfect, but with
God's Direction, You Will Be the Best Momma to Your Children

PART VI
Muting All Mommy Shamers
TRUTH # 6 - Your Awesomeness Can't Be Defined by Others

PART VII
From Worrier to Warrior
TRUTH #7 - You Can Give Up Googling and Look to the Word

PART VIII
Squashing the Scheduling Savages
TRUTH #8 – In Christ You Can Find Rest from
the Parenting Rat Race

PART IX
Adulting: Accept the Challenge. Play by the Rules.
Win at Parenting.
*TRUTH #9 – You Know What's Up with
This Whole Parenting Thing*

PART X
This Too Shall Pass
(Boogers and Poopy Diapers Included)
Truth #10 – You Will Get Through This

Foreword

Anyone reading Erin Brown Hollis' *Cheers to the Diaper Years* will benefit from these wise, good-humored conversations and realize they've found someone who understands the challenges of being a mom. These well-paced pages offer humor-laced experience, but Hollis' best ingredient, missing from so many parenting books, is that mommyhood is a specific divine calling that none of us can do alone. She reminds us that God is with us in our daily joys as well as in the midnight feedings and walk-the-floor bouts of sickness.

Each of the book's ten parts links to a vital truth. Part I opens with "Mommyhood: You Have Been Chosen," which connects to Truth #1, "You Were Selected by God to Be 'Momma' to Your Babies." Those freeing words help defeat our fear of failing by reminding us that God is our guarantor; we are in this role with Him. Truth #2, which links to Part II, adds, "You Are More Than Enough in Christ!" Wonderfully, that means He is more than enough in us!

Cheers to the Diaper Years grew from Erin Brown Hollis' popular website blog that focuses on freeing and uplifting moms. Her messages create a place for ladies to identify and share their journeys and joys. As the childhood nursery rhyme says, "First comes love, then comes marriage, then comes (you) with a baby carriage." Moms look quite different than dazzling prom dates or gorgeous brides coming down the aisle. We spend most of our time in food-stained workout clothes feeding (or wiping) precious little faces—not dressed up for date nights with handsome husbands. Hollis' pages remind us to lean on Christ and encourage others while serving in the trenches where our daily parenting battles are fought and won.

I recommend this book as essential to moms as a favorite morning beverage pick-me-up. Give it as a gift to those needing a smile or a spring in their step while performing sacred mommyhood duties. As Billy Graham's wife, Ruth, understood in co-raising their five children, parenting is a God-given calling. This sign, written in Old English lettering, still hangs above her kitchen sink: "Divine service will be conducted here three times daily." That's three times a day, ladies—three times *every* day. It's in these small segments of loving service, wearing smiles on our faces and spaghetti stains (or worse) on our clothes, where mom-warriors win medals.

As we raise the children God entrusts to us, our most important task is not doing everything right. For Hollis, it has included "reading bedtime stories, playing Barbies, doing puzzles, and snuggling with my two little girls. ... I want my girls to know that they can achieve anything they dream through hard work and God's guidance."

This wise, fun book for those in mommyhood years inspires and encourages us most of all to bask daily in God's love, fellowship, and help, while teaching our children to do the same.

Delores Topliff, *BA, MA, C.Ed.D.*
Professor at the University of Northwestern–St. Paul (MN), college curriculum writer, and international speaker and seminar presenter

Introduction

Dear Reader,
I have a sneaking suspicion we could be soul sisters. Maybe we were even separated at birth. *Who knows?* Only time will tell.

But I know one thing for sure: If you are a mom or on your way to being one … if you are tackling the daily grind of mommin', you are my people. I love you. I understand you. And I am here to represent you if you'll indulge me for a bit.

When I first learned I was pregnant, I shared my joy with my tribe and then, immediately, went to the bookstore to pick up every book imaginable that could teach me how to rock it out in my new role as "Mommy." There are thousands of books out there to show you how to change a diaper, tell you when to wean, and give you reviews about the best baby monitor—*and they're great*—but I needed a book that told me what to do when I was curled up on my bathroom floor doubting my ability to carry on. Try googling "what to do when sitting on the floor of bathroom crying when your kid won't go to sleep."

In case you're wondering, every child requires the following bedtime routine (according to the internet): (1) change diaper or potty; (2) brush teeth; (3) read a book; (4) turn on the nightlight; (5) chase away the boogie man; (6) solve world hunger; and, my personal favorite, (7) discuss every single thing you tried to get her to talk about during the day that she didn't seem hip to discuss over her PB&J at lunchtime. This type of research will take you down a rabbit trail ending in a wild goose chase that will likely never lead you to Christ—*which is exactly where you gotta run, girl.*

So I got a little frustrated with my lack of an instruction manual. Not many authors authentically tackled the battlefield I now know as motherhood. Because if we're being honest about motherhood, it's Crazytown, USA. Population: Every single one of us.

I simply wanted to be heard. I wanted a community of support where I felt comfortable to sometimes commiserate, but all the time celebrate.

My guess is that you are preparing for motherhood, or maybe you are right in the thick of it, like me. No matter how you've arrived at this book, I need to promise you one thing: I'm certainly *not* going to pretend to have this whole thing figured out.

Sure, I could sit here and spell out all the different ways to swaddle your baby, when to soothe, and how to bathe, but someone has already done all of that. This book addresses what I feel to be some real tough-stuff motherhood issues: the things that keep us up at night—outside of the wake-up calls from our precious progeny—like self-doubt, the pressures of being enough, and worry.

Instead of telling you how to live your life, I plan to extend my hand, offer you grace, and hope that at the end of this, we are besties destined to support one another on this crazy, wild journey of motherhood. Picture this book like a good-ole-fashioned girls' night (or naptime escape) where we are going to chat about all the highs and lows of motherhood, followed by a "Cheers!" to the grace and goodness we can find in Christ to embrace each one!

I'm going to let you in on a little secret: Nothing in this book (or any book outside the Bible, for that matter) will solve all our mommy manic moments, but I hope after our time together that you feel heard. I hope you feel community. I hope you feel me reaching out, assuring you that you are not alone. Let's be friends, girl!

I don't want to be known as the "best mom." I want to be known as the best mom for *my* kids. I want to stay up late for dance parties and snuggle in on Saturday mornings. I want to read one book that turns into twenty at bedtime and then recharge with my hubby before the next sleep interruption occurs. I want to soak up the tiny moments—*the ones that matter*.

My second sneaking suspicion is that so do you.

So, with all that being said, my first tip to you is this: Run, don't walk, and stock your freezer with ice cream, your contact list with trustworthy friends, and your heart with the Word. Let's do this, girl. *Together*.

I may not know everything about parenting, but I know the *One* who does.

PART I

Mommyhood: You Have Been Chosen

Mom Confession: I often find myself wondering how I ended up with these precious children who also kind of drive me crazy at times.

CHEERS TO ...

TRUTH #1 – You Were Selected by God to Be "Momma" to Your Babies

Out of all the options in the entire universe, God selected YOU to parent your child(ren).

....

For we are His workmanship, created in Christ Jesus
for good works, which God prepared beforehand
so that we would walk in them.

EPHESIANS 2:10 NASB

1

Calling All Fellow Commandeers of the Hot Mess Express

Mommyhood. *Wow.* What a ride. Actually, it's more like a roller coaster with no seatbelts. Am I right, ladies? So much of parenting is the ability to finally look in the mirror and admit, *Yes. This is my circus. And yes. These are my monkeys.*

Days that end with no trips to the emergency room, anxiety prescriptions, or breakdowns resulting in over-divulging therapy sessions equate to a "W" (Win) on the scoreboard of life for us card-carrying members of the Mommy Club. Take a brief moment and give yourself a pat on the back if you are headed toward another "W" on the board for today.

Sometimes we just need to locate and resonate with women going through the exact same highs and lows we are experiencing. We yearn to find our tribe.

If you are a momma, *this* is your tribe. Welcome home.

This book is meant to serve as a perma-hug, a handshake, a high-five, a pat on the back, an air kiss on each cheek, and a star on your reward chart. Whatever your preferred salutation for love recognition happens to be, that's what this book is intended to provide. It's a reminder that we're all in this together. Every single one of us. We are *worthy* in Christ. We are *strong*. We are *chosen*.

So get comfy, grab a blanket, turn off the TV (yep, even that awesome guilty pleasure kind—I promise we can catch the DVR version later), and grab your favorite beverage of choice. Let's curl up on the couch, like the two besties we are going to be by the end of our time together, and chat. Buckle up, mommas. Let's talk mommyhood!

Let's start with the most important message of all: Being a mom is the most significant earthly gift *and* calling we could ever receive. Parenting is a privilege that many of us spend years praying and dreaming about. We pray to receive the blessing of a child. We pray for them once they arrive. Sometimes we pray for them to go away (joking!—kinda). It seems like we pray every single moment of the day for these divine gifts! And they really *are* gifts. God's Word tells us so: "Children are a blessing and a gift from the LORD" (Psalm 127:3 CEV).

Children are absolute blessings, no doubt about it. In fact, I would bet that if you've ever experienced the sheer elation of parenting a child, you know what I mean. Their first breath. The first time that teeny-tiny hand grasps your finger. Those first steps. All. The. Heart. Eyes. Friends, life would not be the same without their embrace and innocent eyes reminding us of this precious gift we call life. Take note of these warm and fuzzy feelings you are having right now. We will need to be feeling those later on when we delve off into #RealTalk.

As parents, we really should thank God frequently throughout the day for the honor and privilege of His entrustment of our little ones. And consider *this* humbling fact with me for a hot second: Out of every single option in the world, God chose *you* to be the parent of *your* child(ren).

He did not select your mother-in-law.

He did not select your friend with her Pinterest-perfect, country-club-chic, yoga-obsessed, clean-eating, seemingly lovely life.

He did not even select that nosy lady in the produce section at the grocery store who always seems to have all the answers to parenting. Nope. Nuh-uh. God chose *you*! He hand-selected *you* (am I emphasizing this enough? I'm talking to you, girlfriend!) to love them, encourage them, and guide them along their journey(s) of life. No one on earth could do a better job than you! (Not even Reese Witherspoon. Even though, let's be real, we all wish we could be her kid. Or her best friend. Or just her acquaintance. "Reese, can we be friends? Check yes __ or no __." Moving on …)

From the moment we learn we are going to be moms, an innate drive awakens in our souls. This all-consuming urge to learn everything we can about our new adventure takes over. And *then*, we delve off into the world of research. We google more than ever before. We reach out to every nook and cranny of the internet, hunting for the latest rules of the game. We subscribe to every mommy blog available. We call every friend who has ever even thought about birthing a child. Honestly, we should receive PhDs for how proficient we become in the field of domestication. And the advice just floods in, doesn't it?

I wish there was a way we could turn off "mommy notifications" in our brains, much like the options in social media these days to spare us the incessant intrusion of even more "mommy deets." There must be some way we can enjoy a moment of peace on the journey of motherhood!

Once baby arrives, we enter a state of uncharted euphoria—you know, after recovering from that moment of wondering whether or not our body just literally exploded. As our little one is placed in our arms, we stare into this tiny face, and for a brief moment it's just perfection. Just the two (or three or five or insert number of your applicable children here) of us. It's all good in the 'hood. This precious little thing has been entrusted to us. We love all the cuddles, the coos, and the cute faces. We eat up those tender moments and catalog them in our brains for generations to come.

And it's all fun and Instagram-worthy moments, until we head into our new reality. That wheelchair ride down to the car is like a gigantic backhand across the face and shove off the edge of the Grand Canyon into the Abyss of Adulting. (In case you're curious, I capitalized the word *Adulting* because it's a real place, y'all.) We cling to the car door like we're being kidnapped and forced into uncomfortable servitude. And it takes everything inside of us not to turn around and scream, "Sweet, precious, beautiful nurse, who hasn't left my side in two days, come home with me!"

Jesus, be an at-home baby nurse.

Those first few hours back home after leaving the hospital are, well, like discovering a whole new world—*not* to be confused with the Aladdin-and-Jasmine version. Think the Beast's castle (fight-scene style) or the battlefield in *Mulan.* And what about the thirty minutes after our family and friends leave our side for the first time to tend to their *own* lives once again?

Then the fun *really* begins.

We can all agree on one thing: Babies are *not* born with handbooks, schedules, and lists of their needs tied to their tiny ankles as they enter this world—*disappointing, I know.* There is no roadmap to parenting. There is no manual explaining how to feed an infant who appears to have been born with aversions to any and all forms of nourishment. There is no pamphlet describing how to adequately clean poop used as finger paint on a crib. (Am I the only one raising a future Poop van Gogh? Say it ain't so!) There are no rules to assist in teaching your toddler *not* to swim in the toilet. And, sadly, there is no game plan designed to scare away the boogie man at 4:00 a.m.

Remember how I suggested earlier to soak up those precious moments of tenderness and Instagram perfection and burn them into your memory? Okay, good. Close your eyes and picture those for a bit. Yeah, get all that light-of-a-thousand-fairies dancing in your head. *You good?* All right, moving on.

In addition to the over-the-moon moments, there are also times we want to run in the street and vigilantly wave our arms until someone whisks us away from our current reality and plops us in an alternate one. Of silence. And cleanliness. And *freedom*.

There will be moments when we look in the mirror and doubt our ability to carry on. Girl, I so feel you. There are moments when we feel overwhelmed, overworked, and undervalued (feels like a "can I get an amen?" moment). We will feel defeated and not up to the task, but so long as we remember to cling to the promise we just discussed—that we were chosen for this—there's a reassuring feeling of God's provision that washes over us. "His divine power has given us everything we need for a godly life through our knowledge of him who called us by his own glory and goodness" (2 Peter 1:3).

That's what this book is all about—finding hope when we feel there is none. Getting a hug when we feel like we are invisible. And reminding ourselves that we are all in this together.

Love you, sister. Time to let it all hang out and conquer all these issues together.

2

A Cautionary Tale

would like to continue our time together by sharing a cautionary tale. And not to go all Savage Garden (circa 1997) on you, but it's one that I feel *truly, madly, deeply* about.

First, let's get to know one another.

Hey, y'all! I'm Erin. I am a mommy to two girls, a wife to one man (ha! I feel weird typing it that way, but surely Marshall will appreciate the numeric accuracy, right?), a daughter to the two greatest folks on the planet, and a sister to a guy who deserves it all—and then some.

I always find it roll-on-the-floor laughable when people assume that I have it "together." I guess my reputation for being a sassy dresser with a penchant for a bold lip precedes me and disguises my true soul mates in life: *sweatpants* and *spaghetti stains*. Alert the elders, folks, because this Pinterest Princess persona is an outright fallacy. I try. I really, really do. But I mess it up *so* much of the time.

As an attorney, I feel obligated to provide you a little evidence to serve as proof. Here goes …

I totaled my first car at sixteen years old—fifty-eight days after receiving it, even though my dad prognosticated that I had a solid sixty days before phoning him up from a ditch on the side of the highway somewhere. (I'm all about beating out those benchmarks, people!)

I invited boys over to my house at eighteen years old when my parents were three hours away on vacation, even though they warned me for weeks that if I did, I'd never see the light of day again. (Somehow I escaped being found out, even though I'm currently huddled up at a local library, in the dark, typing to my new besties—you!—so potato, po-tah-toe with the whole light-of-day thing, I guess.)

I ran for Student Government Association president against the most popular guy in school my senior year of high school and received two (*two!*) votes: myself and my brother. (*Wait, Brad, did you vote for me?!*) Needless to say, my concession speech was akin to a good-ole-fashioned dumpster fire. Good times. Gooooood times.

Is anyone noticing a trend here?

At some point, I began to question if God was planning to use this wannabe achiever. The girl who had big dreams but needed a little structured vision due to her penchant for epic fails.

Then I turned twenty-seven and found out my husband and I were expecting. I was finally going to knock it out of the park, friends. I was going to be Mommy of the Year! (Ha! Sorry. I'm pausing to collect myself because I just disturbed a whole table of nearby studiers in this library by laughing out loud at my own ~~idiocy~~ gentle naivety.)

Like many of you with kids, I immediately thought I knew more than every single mother who had ever given birth. I'm lookin' at you, Eve. (I know I'm better than you. No snake is gonna steal my focus from achieving Mommy of the Year!)

I say all of this even though in the first few weeks of my baby's existence, I found myself rocking back and forth on the bed for hours each night, freaking out about whether or not I should offer my baby a pacifier because the judgy momspert (mom + expert) guides had scolded me against it.

Within moments of my baby's birth, I was forcing that boob right on her. You know, because "society" told me that was what I was supposed to do. Spoiler Alert: She didn't take it and ended up on the BiliBed with severe jaundice for three days. And I asked God, "What is my purpose? I can't breastfeed, so what do I do now?!"

Cut to a year later, and there was that time when my toddler painted her entire crib with her own poop, even though I had *just* explained to her that feces have not been deemed an art medium even in our super-open-minded modern age—because sixteen-month-olds are wildly interested in the history and trends of uppity culture today. I cocked my head right back up at God and said, "What is my purpose? I can't even keep my kid from exploring her van-Gogh-esque qualities with her own waste!"

So yeah. God has a way of grounding us, doesn't He?

#RealTalk: I'm a momma just like you. I have moments when I knock this mom-gig right outta the park, and then I have my moments when I think God must have been kidding when He placed these little lovebugs in my care.

But then it hit me: God was utilizing these vulnerable "I don't have a clue what I'm supposed to be doing" moments in my life to draw me back to my *true* purpose: loving Him, doing my best to model Christ's forgiveness, and extending His grace to everyone I meet—including myself.

Here comes a #TruthBomb: Our purpose on this earth is *not* defined by our parenting journey. Our purpose on this earth is to lead others to Christ, to live as Jesus did, and to strive day in and day out to be more like Him. "We are here to bring glory and honor to God. We're here at the Father's good pleasure. We're here *on* purpose, *for* a purpose—His purpose."[1]

Cheers. To. That.

....

Our purpose on this earth is *not* defined by our parenting journey.

....

It seems that now more than ever we find ourselves searching for our purpose, looking for that *one* thing God has set us on this earth to accomplish. And I think we get confused with the terms *purpose* and *calling*. When we confuse those two, it can send us down a never-ending rabbit trail of disappointment. Our *purpose* is to love God with our heart, soul, and mind (Matthew 22:37–38). One of our *callings* is to lovingly guide our precious babies into the arms of Christ (Proverbs 22:6).

When we remind ourselves that our purpose on this earth is not limited to our parenting, we free ourselves from the shame and disappointment that will come with everyday mothering and open ourselves up to the paths God has chosen for each of us. "Motherhood isn't a means to fulfilling our need for purpose, but an outpouring of living full in the spirit. The secret to finding your purpose is simply finding more of God."[2] When we start looking at motherhood as one of the vessels to *reveal* our purpose, everything seems much more meaningful and, frankly, *doable*.

Have you ever found yourself saying this little ditty: "God designed me to be a mommy"? Yes, my friend, He did! But He also designed you for something even greater—to reach *your* people, *your* tribe, and *your* world with the hope and grace we have in Christ! When we focus on serving God, we are allowing Him to shine through *every* aspect of our lives, not just limiting Him to our home address, our babies, our church, or our backyards. Instead, we are saying, "God, use me in this home. Use me at the grocery store. Use me in the boardroom. Use me at this restaurant. Use me *everywhere*."

The most incredible moment in my parenting journey came when I realized that God actually did *not* pick me to be *the* Mommy of the Year. God chose me to be *a* mom. And what we are going to learn together is to thank the good Lord for that simple fact.

I am not a child psychologist. I do not have a PhD in early childhood education. And aren't we glad? Because honestly, I don't understand what those well-meaning souls are saying half the time anyway (love you though, experts!). I am a *real* mom writing to *real* moms. I do not know everything there is to know about motherhood—*but I know the One who does.*

Okay. Awesome. I'm so glad we know each other better, because this journey is gonna get bumpy before it gets great. Back to my cautionary tale.

God did not choose *you* to be Mommy of the Year either. Hallelujah. Praise God! And all the mommies said, "Amen." He chose you to be a mom by gifting you with the blessing of a child. And not just any old mom. He chose *you* to be the mom to *your* kids. Girlfriend, being a mom is the most incredible thing you could ever do with your life. The other incredible thing is that not a single one of us will ever do this mom thing perfectly. So here is my one word of caution: from this point forward, run from anything that teaches you otherwise! Hide yo kids and hide yoself from any book, blog, person, robot, website, car salesman, grocery-store cashier, old-lady neighbor, meddling mother-in-law, or long-lost bestie from high school who claims that he or she can coach you into (rather, shame you into) being the perfect mom. Instead, just fall into the arms of Christ. The best thing you can do is learn how to *thrive* in this whole motherhood game rather than *perfect* it, because there's nobody perfect but God Himself.

Well, we've been curled up on the couch for a bit now, chatting it up. And I gotta say, I am loving this time we are sharing. We're friends now, right? (I'm over here unashamedly looking for that good-ole-fashioned friend request, girl. *Just sayin'.*) Promise me you'll never forget this: You can totally do this job called "Mom." You are strong, and you are capable. In fact, you were *chosen* for such a time as this.

3

What Somebody Should *Actually* Tell Us When We Are Expecting

Now that we have established that we are chosen for this awesome role of Mommy, I want to make a confession. When I took my precious firstborn home from the hospital on a chilly fall day back in 2012, I had not one clue what to do with that sweet (and boisterous) bundle of joy. I felt like they probably shouldn't have let me leave the premises. Looking back, I'm not exactly sure what caused Brookwood Hospital's staff to make the decision to send us home. (I'm guessing my incessant requests for lime-margarita-flavored popsicles every fifteen minutes might have had something to do with it, but the jury is still out on all that.)

Once we arrived home and took all the mandatory "we're home!" memory-making scrapbook pictures, I began my nesting drills (only six-ish months late to that party). I dug my hand down into a bag the hospital ever-so-generously gifted me with at our departure ceremony, hunting for the instruction manual to guide me in nurturing my newest prized possession. And would you believe, they left mine out? They let me leave that hospital with not a single guide explaining what to do with my brand-new baby! So it made me very reflective on this scary notion of babies leaving hospitals with well-meaning yet woefully unprepared parental units.

When you show up to a car dealership and buy a car, it comes with a manual. Cookbooks come with long, drawn-out recipes that include intense instructions. Doctor appointments do not commence until you've read an encyclopedia full of disclaimers, the love story surrounding the origination of HIPAA, and the latest educational/athletic achievements of the doctor's kids. Heck, even purchasing a cell phone requires reviewing a seventy-five-page document these days.

So why in the world do babies not come with instruction manuals tied ever-so-neatly to their tiny ankles?

It seems like the most important responsibility in the world should come with a little more prep. Just sayin'. *Do you hear me, God? It's Erin …*

Instead of flipping through a handy-dandy CliffsNotes version of motherhood, I read *all* the books about what to do, what not to do, how to do it, and how not to do it. My head is still spinning from all that research, actually. And while reading that *What to Expect When You're Expecting* book is great and all, I wish somebody had taken a few moments for some #RealTalk with your girl and shared the following things.

God (and our babies) will still love us, even when we burn dinner

I gotta tell you, the pressure to be "enough" has never been greater in our world. And sometimes (read: *all* the time), I just wanna let my crazy hang out, and I'd be willing to bet you do too. If we set this unrealistic standard for ourselves, especially when it comes to mommyhood, what does that say to our kids? That they have to live up to those standards too?! Whoa now. I'm scared just thinking about that. It's a simple statistical fact of life that we're gonna burn dinner, and we're gonna lose our kid in Target at least once, maybe twice. (If more than twice, maybe consider seeing somebody about that. But no judgment, promise.)

Thank goodness that our God is not in the business of a *second*

CHEERS TO THE DIAPER YEARS

chance. He is in the business of *another* chance. And we get another chance every single day. Wouldn't life be super boring if the washing machine spilling soap suds all over the kitchen floor *wasn't* the opening line at every Christmas dinner? It will not be funny in the moment, but the moments that our society has oh-so-lovingly dubbed "epic fails" actually become the spice of life, the watercooler stand-up-comic moments, and the memory-book fillers.

So you do you, Momma. Let it all hang out. Some days you might be worthy of the cover story in *Good Housekeeping*. Others you won't. But don't forget to celebrate both. Strive to be your best, but always land in your truth. Because God is there. And that's where you need to be too.

Motherhood is the greatest joy and toughest challenge of your life

If someone had told me that within an hour of my first child's birth, I would have to decide to change pediatricians, figure out whether or not to put her on the BiliBed, agonize over breastfeeding, and shoo away unwelcomed commentary from the peanut gallery, I might have prepared myself a whole lot better for the journey.

We don't really get a heads up that motherhood is actually *not* so much about planning all the playdates, but rather about piling on heaps of God's grace. It's about owning the fact that we *don't* know everything, and running into the arms of the One who does. It's about recognizing the moments we need help, asking for it, and extending it to others when they need it too.

Which leads me to …

No mother knows more about your kids than you do

As it turns out, every person in the world has an opinion about every other person in the world. Some of these "opinions" are good and some are bad. Some are legit. Some are malicious. Some are just concocted bull … Well, you know what I mean. And, unfortunately, these opinions do not always remain confidential. Especially when it comes to motherhood, for some reason.

Mommy shaming is alive and well, friends. And if you think you're exempt from its unassuming death grip of terribleness, think again. It may present itself in the form of a well-meaning "suggestion" from a friend or, even worse, from an in-law (dun, dun, dun …). Or it may come in the form of a tacky comment on social media that hits you like a snake bite in the wilderness of Mommy Mayhem. But, however it manifests, I've got good news. Unless the arbiter of this ill-advised commentary either assisted in the procreation of your offspring or is God Himself, tell that hater to take several seats.

In the past, I have been guilty of succumbing to upset feelings when someone spewed her venom my way. But then I realized that God had not selected that individual to parent my child. He had not chosen *her* to nurture, guide, and love my little ones. So what did her opinion matter when it came to my child or my parenting? Spoiler Alert: It doesn't matter one bit. The old saying goes there can be "too many cooks in the kitchen." Well, there can be too many mommas in the nursery as well, folks.

We don't really get a heads up that motherhood is actually *not* so much about planning all the playdates, but rather about piling on heaps of God's grace.

So, here's a heads up: Don't allow anyone to steal your joy. Seek God's confidence and rest in His grace. You are never going to be perfect, but with His direction, you will be the best momma to *your* child. Just as He designed it in the first place.

Pinterest is straight from satan

Can someone show me the Scripture that says I must send personalized invitations printed on heavy-duty card stock for my child's first birthday party? Like, where did Jesus frown upon Evite? Or Paperless Post? Or heck, even a group text? (*Maybe it's in the footnotes?*) Mom Confession: I have a love/hate (*despise*) relationship with Pinterest, because who realistically has time to raise children, keep house, potentially work, actively participate in a marriage, *and* make butterfly-shaped tofu-kale burgers with spinach and avocado tater tots?!

Really though. I'm being serious. Present yourself. We need to have a long chat, because this is about to be the momma movie version of *[S]he's Just Not That Into You*. I'm the Bradley Cooper character over here looking for the "fun" ones, and Pinterest-Perfect Girl ain't making that cut. #GoAndTellThat. While you are donning your no-doubt freshly ironed, monogrammed apron, whipping up homemade non-GMO treats, and creating Pulitzer-Prize-worthy handmade baby books, I am struggling to find the missing sippy cup that has two-week-old milk still in it.

And guess what? I am *now* totally okay with that, because one day I really am going to spend hours crafting and wearing my "DIY Diva" label with pride. I mean, who *doesn't* want those gorgeous white marble countertops with pristine mason jars spilling over with home-grown succulents. But for now, I will leave the Pinterest Perfection game to others, and you'll find me over here with my kiddos making memories while rolling around in piles of laundry that we aren't even completely sure are clean or dirty at the moment.

Mamaste, friends. Mamaste.

Never say never

I'll never forget sitting in a restaurant at the age of eighteen, glaring at a mother feverishly attempting to maintain three little ones. I was so ticked off that these tiny rugrats were ruining my night out on the town.

Cut to twelve years later when I swallowed an entire humble pie as my three-year-old threw herself onto the floor of that *same* restaurant, kicking and screaming while about thirty patrons stared at me with a "Get the heck outta here!" look of derision. God sure does have a sense of humor. And I honestly think that when we make little comments like "I would *never* let my kids do that" or "That would *never* happen on my watch," He somehow always finds a way to make us eat that crow.

Heads up: The paci that just fell on the wood floor into a pile of sticky three-day-old crumbs may *have* to be inserted into your infant's mouth, *pre*-boiling and intense cleansing, to preserve you and your baby's sanity. Even though you swore up and down you would *never* allow it to happen.

There's that word again.

You've been warned.

If you've been on the fence about the word tribe, *jump off the fence and find yours, like now—you will need them to survive*

Where my boos at? Love you forever, #SoulSisters! If there is one thing I have learned along this whole parenting journey, it's that next to your own biological mother, there is *no one* who understands you more on this earth than another mother.

We (mothers) are bound by a common bond that transcends all understanding.

We get each other in the most intimate of ways. I mean, with who else can you discuss cramping, discharge, and poo-poo patrol while simultaneously not fearing righteous condemnation and/or total alienation? I can be standing in line at the grocery store, catch the eye of a fellow mom, and it's like an instant "I see you, sister" moment. Have you ever had that happen?

When I put my kids in ballet, I decided to start mom-dating, and I was looking for a lifer, not a one-night stand. (Anybody feel me on this?) No, I'm not referencing infidelity, unless of course, you consider my borderline obsessively intense relationship with my tribe as infidelity.

Moving on …

Boy, did I find my girls, and I have dug my claws into them ever since. At 3:00 a.m., when I just can't take it anymore, the return text message that reads "Girl, ME TOO! Baby threw up AGAIN!" is honestly more comforting than a two-hour uninterrupted massage.

If you have not located your tribe, girl, do it today. And I'll be the first member, if you'll have me.

There is no purer form of love than a slobbery kiss at 2:00 a.m.

If I could bottle up the sweetness that I experience with my little ones in the wee hours of the morning, I would. Because years from now when my schedule is freer and those same babies are out there conquering their own little worlds, I will be missing all the late-night chats, bedtime stories, and bath battles.

There really is an intoxicating greatness found in those bear hugs and slobbery kisses from your child. Make time for each of them. Soak up every single one, because as we will learn later, these really *are* the days, friends.

The rest of our time will be spent exploring these revelations and learning what *God* has to say about this whole motherhood thing. As it turns out, the manual we've been searching for was on our night-stands all along. The better we arm ourselves with God's grace and fill our hearts with His Word, the more prepared we will be from now on to celebrate all the wonderful days and the not-so-wonderful ones.

CHEERS TO ...

- 🦆 Reminding yourself that you have been chosen for this journey called mommyhood.
- 🦆 Knowing that your babies are gifts from God, and you are #Blessed.
- 🦆 Celebrating the truth that no one can take your place as "Mom."

🦆 Today's Celebration: Take a second to look at your babies and thank God for them. Thank Him for choosing you to be the driver of your very own Hot Mess Express. Remind your children that you are so thankful God chose you to be their mom and that you will love, nurture, and protect them always through Christ who gives you strength.

🦆 I encourage you to pick a real-life photo (not a posed one for your next holiday card), one where you are laughing/hugging/snuggling/rolling around on spaghetti-stained couch cushions with your kiddos. Consider framing that photo and placing it on your nightstand. Each morning, take one second to glance at that photo and remind yourself why being a mommy to your babies truly is the greatest role in the world.

Wow. You are awesome. Do you need a nap before we move on? Friend, I feel you. But come back soon so we can delve deeper into why you, in Christ, are so awesome, and how you can rock it out at this thing called motherhood.

PART II

You Do You—Free Yourself from the Chains of Keeping Up and Embrace the New (Non-Perfect) Mom Inside

Mom Confession: Sometimes (read: *a lot* of the time) I don't feel worthy or capable or even cut out for this whole mommy thing. My home is not going to be on the cover of *Good Housekeeping*, my thighs disqualify me for *America's Next Top Model*, and sometimes it bothers me that Susie Homemaker always seems up to the task for all those things and then some.

CHEERS TO ...

TRUTH #2 – You Are More Than Enough in Christ

Comparing yourself to other moms will only tear you down and cause unnecessary feelings of discouragement. Be proud of who you are in Christ! Who knows, someone may be secretly watching all your moves and learning from your own unique level of awesomeness!

....

> "But blessed is the one who trusts in the LORD,
> whose confidence is in him."
>
> JEREMIAH 17:7

4

Smashing the Stepford Wife Syndrome

I want you all to know that on January 1st of this year, I proclaimed to the world (in other words, the four people sitting in my den at the time) that I was going to eat only healthy foods for the entire year. I would also like you to know that on January 2nd, at approximately 5:17 p.m., I ordered a Papa John's Favorite with extra cheese and, quite honestly, lived my best life. Disclaimer: I did use a 25-percent-off coupon and drank water, though, so #Winning!

While we are traveling down this pathway of truth, I would like you to know a few other things.

When you enter my front door, there is a very good chance you will trip over my child's riding toy or latest Cheerio "experiment." I also need you to understand that there is a high likelihood you will discover a pair of underwear, a rogue donut, or a Barbie head tucked between my couch cushions while we sit and attempt to discuss life. As a side note, if you *do* discover that Barbie head, please help a sister out and let me know, because my little one has been looking for that thing for years!

There's no telling where we will find it though. In fact, not long ago my brother babysat for me and unearthed a fermented waffle in our playroom. Our guesstimation is that it had resided there for at least six months prior to its discovery. You know, hand to heaven, I just wanted to get out of the house to re-engage my sanity only to return home to my very own compost pile—oh well. Hooray! An herb garden always tends to find its way on my New Year's resolution list, so cheers to being ahead this year!

My favorite meal is a juicy cheeseburger, Ruffles potato chips, and a big ole dollop of french onion dip. Sure, you will catch me ordering a token salad from time to time, but don't you dare forget to bring me a bucket of ranch dressing to douse it in.

I don't iron my clothes or anyone else's for that matter. Most people's main priority when picking out a new frock is style. Mine is "Does this tag say, 'Wash with like colors?'" Because if it does, we are good to go, and I can hang that bad boy up the second it leaves the washing machine or more likely toss it on the floor, like the pilgrims did, to keep it moving. I've got babies to chase and bills to pay and that fluorescent mac and cheese isn't gonna stir itself, people!

Speaking of laundry, my dining room is *not* for eating anymore, so please avoid asking me why there are hanging racks decorating all the empty wall space. Unless you are a momma rookie, you should be well aware that dining rooms turn into secondary laundry stations the minute your child is officially delivered into this world.

And, finally, *yes*, you are correct. Cheddar Bunnies and apple sauce squeeze packs *are* now the only "appetizers" I carry up in here, so please check back in approximately sixteen years from now for my locally famous attempt at a charcuterie board.

These are the cold, hard facts, folks!

And while I'm still on the honest train, I'll admit that sometimes these aspects of my "enough-ness," or seeming lack thereof, have me in my emotions just a bit. But listen, if you can't handle me in my Britney Spears (circa baby riding in her lap while driving down the highway) phase, then you don't deserve me at my Reese Witherspoon (circa taking over the world) phase.

And every mother in the world said, "Amen."

Mom Confession: I am *not* a Stepford wife. I do not *want* to be one either. My guess is that nobody's got time for all that jazz anyway! "Living transparently—as God's broken beloved—is contagious. When we are honest about our brokenness, those around us will be inspired to do the same. They will be freed to be honest about how fragile they feel. That is how we use our brokenness to bless others."[3]

The most beautiful people I know on this earth are *not* turning down phone calls for the cover of *Vogue*. What I'm trying to communicate is that my favorite people in life are *not* my favorite people in life because they can rock a good suede wedge in the summer, prepare a meal rivaling that of the Barefoot Contessa, and strut a runway better than Kendall Jenner. Quite the contrary, actually. They are my friends because they shine that beautiful light of Christ wherever they go.

They bring meals when I am ill. They love on my babies as if they are their own. They extend a hug at just the right time as well as provide me distance when necessary. They don't judge my laundry piles and instead sit and help me fold my socks. They are my favorites because they feed my soul, day in and day out, with the simple reminder that God is good—*all the time*.

As I'm maturing, I'm finding myself much less interested in pursuing long-lasting skin care and much more interested in long-lasting *soul* care. Sure, I wanna look alive and all, but if all that people have to say about me on my final day is, "That girl and her home always looked so good," then I've outright failed at this whole Christian-living thing.

The other night, I was out with some of my fellow mommas, you know, on our monthly momma survival dinner, and a name of a mutual friend came up in conversation. I watched as each momma went on and on about how "precious" she was, or how "thoughtful" she always seemed to be. Then one of my friends took it a step further, and her words have rocked my world. She said, "I love her so much because I have never met anyone who so beautifully displays the fruits of the Spirit."

Mic-drop moment.

Forget about having a pristine entryway and the most scrumptious treats. I want people to remember me for being gentle, joyful, and kind. I sat there in shock as I totally re-evaluated my priorities. I want you to know that this same friend is *not* known for her perfectionism, but rather by the grace she extends to everyone, including herself.

"But the fruit of the Spirit is love, joy, peace, forbearance, kindness, goodness, faithfulness, gentleness and self-control. Against such things there is no law. Those who belong to Christ Jesus have crucified the flesh with its passions and desires. Since we live by the Spirit, let us keep in step with the Spirit" (Galatians 5:22–25).

Do you see any mention of the ability to bake Pioneer-Woman-approved peach pies in that verse above? Because I didn't run across that quality above either.

You might be saying, "Wait a minute, Erin! What about the Proverbs 31 woman? Aren't we supposed to model our lives after *that* level of Boss Lady?" My answer is twofold based off research:

1. Absolutely, we need to aspire to Proverbs 31 status, but it is very clear to me after rereading Proverbs 31 that this woman was *not* setting out to win the town's pie-baking contest every week or receiving accolades for the cleanest baseboards. In fact, we don't have proof she even cared about silly little titles like that. *This* woman worked with eager hands (v. 13); provided for her family (v. 15); opened her arms to those in need (v. 20); was clothed in strength and dignity (v. 25); spoke with wisdom (v. 26); and watched over her affairs (v. 27), among other things. Note that perfection was never mentioned. She was a hard

worker, a noble woman, and interested in chasing after a life filled with Christ. Which leads me to number 2.

2. Our primary goal should be to live like Christ. If we focus our attention on pleasing *Him* rather than living up to the fleeting ideals of our society, we will find ourselves in line with God's *real* plan for our lives. And just in case some of us are not completely convinced about this whole "stop chasing perfection" game, allow me to include this verse for our consideration: "For all have sinned and fall short of the glory of God, and all are justified freely by his grace through the redemption that came by Christ Jesus" (Romans 3:23–24).

So yeah, we can chase this whole "Stepford-wife level of awesomeness" thing all day long, friend. But it's a "carrot at the end of a stick" game that we will never quite reach. Side Note: After reading this chapter, does anybody else have TLC's song "Don't Go Chasing Waterfalls" permanently emblazoned in their heads right now? Because if not, well, now you do. *You're welcome.*

> If we focus our attention on pleasing *Him* rather than living up to the fleeting ideals of our society, we will find ourselves in line with God's *real* plan for our lives.

We will all be remembered for something. Rather than being remembered for my crumb-free kitchen floors, I pray I am remembered for loving my babies, living for Christ, and giving everything I have to serve others. Instead of chasing the benchmarks of the quintessential Stepford-wife perfection, follow me to the next chapter, where we are going to learn to run toward the fruits of the Spirit and into the waiting arms of Christ. Because *that* is where we are going to find all the enough-ness we could ever need.

5

Picture-Perfect Performance— and the Other Lies Instagram Tells Us

am a member of an online Facebook mommy group. It consists of an open thread where any of us can post anything, at any time, with the sole purpose of helping a fellow sister out. Questions such as "What is the best playground in town?" or "Where do you ladies shop for post-maternity, mommy-belly clothes?" are tossed around on the regular. Every now and then, we get a spicy one that can lead to some wild discussions, creating an opportunity for us to show grace—or not.

One such moment occurred recently, when a mom posted a seemingly innocent question: "How much one-on-one time do you ladies spend with your kid daily?" She went on to graciously explain that she was feeling a little guilty because she wasn't sure if she spent enough time with hers.

Responses such as these began pouring in: "I always devote two and a half hours to one-on-one time followed by reading and snuggling." And "We make mealtimes special and always do a learning segment in the afternoons." The poor girl had *just* stated that she felt self-conscious about the lack of time she spent with her kids, and out came the Model Mommy Mob to make her feel even more self-conscious.

Do you have any interest in *my* response?

This will let you in a little bit on my psyche. I responded (verbatim): "Here's a tip for at least one hour: Buy a karaoke machine. No joke. Santa brought mine one for Christmas with microphones, and every day at a random time (normally the second before I literally lose my cool), I scream, 'Does everyone know what time it is?', and they scream back, 'Dance party!' Then I put them in a room and let them go to town for like an hour.

"Yes. It is loud and obnoxious at times. But the door is closed, they are pacified exerting energy, and honestly, my kids can sing 'Defying Gravity,' 'Fight Song,' and several rap-ish songs (along with all our favorite Sunday school songs, of course!).

"*Score!* I figure, I am expanding their musical palettes (is that even a thing?), and who doesn't want their kids showing off their musical repertoire by rapping Diddy in the Publix checkout line?! At the same time, I can usually do a load of laundry, clean the dishes, and catch up on emails. So everyone wins. #Survivor."

I later edited my comment to inform readers that my almost-four-year-old was currently belting "Some Nights," by Fun, and living her best life.

I'm going be so real with you right now—keeping right in line with the tone and focus of this book, might I add: There have been times when I have donned the apron, packed the perfect lunches with the delightful little notes (that my four-year-old can't even read—insert eyeroll here), strutted in the Emily-Post-approved sky-high stilettos, and rocked it out at all the PTO functions.

Then there have been times when I barely made it to carpool line to pick my kids up on time from school. Or left their lunches at home. Or, God forbid, wore pajamas for three straight weeks in a row (okay, the whole year, but who's lookin' anyway?). I'm here to tell you, we all survived in *all* those scenarios. And you know what? My kids loved me the same no matter what I did.

Our babies are not keeping little black books hidden under their mattresses, cataloging all our triumphs and epic-fail missteps. They aren't jotting down whether we got around to hanging their artwork in pristine Joanna-Gaines-approved frames over the perfectly dusted piano in the hallway. And, lest we forget, they aren't even sure how to spell their own names yet, so who are they to tell us that our burned muffins are offensive to them anyway!?

That leads us to our truth-bomb moment of the day: Our quest for super-mommy status actually has *nothing* to do with our kids. It's all about *us*, and *our* need to be recognized for our inherent awesomeness.

Ouch. People, I am slapping my own wrist right now. Trust and believe, friends. Track with me here—we are in this together.

Most of us are members of the participation-trophy generation. Our whole lives, we have been taught to work harder, live better, and strive for more, knowing and *expecting* that recognition would swiftly follow. And even if we don't win, we know that cookie-cutter "you did it, girl!" trophy is headed home with us. We want to win all the awards, and even our popularity is now determined by how many social media "likes" we receive—thank the good Lord our social media prowess and bookshelves full of trophies (or lack thereof) mean diddly squat to our Savior.

I happen to think your Pinterest-perfect homemade burlap wreath is swoon worthy. But I *also* think your failed attempt at homemade granola is delightful too, because it means you tried. And, if I'm being honest, it warms my soul to know that I'm not alone in the whole granola-fail game.

When no one else recognizes the 3:00 a.m. feedings, the hundreds of daily diaper changes, the bath battles, the boo-boo kisses, and the cooking of fourteen different options to finally please Junior, just know that it *is* recognized because *God* is watching every second of the day. So, as long as your children are healthy, safe, and you are raising him/her with the love and instruction of Christ, you are good. In fact, you are *amazing*. Strike that. *God* is amazing through you.

The problem rears its head when we buy into this millennial philosophy of "you are enough." While that phrase sounds empowering, gives us all the feels, and looks trendy splattered all over our Instagram feeds, it's just *not* true. We try feebly to rely on our *own* power rather than clinging to God's power *through* us.

There is no way we can manage this motherhood game, or anything really, on our own, *without* Christ. We are leaving Him entirely out of the picture when we masquerade around in this cloak of awesomeness that the "Boss Babes" of the world so desperately want us to wear. If you want to delve further off into this topic, check out the warning we got about this in 2 Timothy 4:3–5, but as NBC's weekly crime show, *Dateline*, reminds us, #Don't~~Watch~~ReadAlone.

If we were enough, we wouldn't need Christ. We wouldn't need the cross. We wouldn't need salvation. But, as proof of our imperfections, Jesus came and died, nailed our epic fails to the cross, and redeemed us through His immeasurable grace and love. Our *inadequacies* actually highlight the *adequacy* of Christ. Recognizing our reliance on Christ parks us in a state of humility and acceptance of Christ as our enoughness. And *that's* the kind of "enough" I want up in my life, friend.

However, if we live our lives based on the lie that we possess everything it takes to succeed and be happy, and the ability to make it all work, we push out the only One who *is* enough. When we are preoccupied with listening to the noise of the world—the ones who tell us about our own enough-ness—we will most certainly lose out on the intimate reception we need to have with our Savior—the One who saved us from perfection posturing in the first place.

Sure, we don't feel a need for Him when everything's perfect, dinner was delicious, and the kids are bathed and in bed on time, but what about when things aren't so perfect? The worst part of this belief is that by holding ourselves out as the "hero," we have no one to turn to when we realize we really *do* need help at the end of the day. When the car won't start. When the pasta boils over. When our child gets sick. When the hubby travels too much.

I love the way Lara Casey addresses this in her book *Cultivate*: "You have likely heard the popular phrase: 'She believed she could, so she did.' Those words are lovely and instill confidence, but it doesn't last. I know a deeper truth: *she believed she couldn't, so He did.* You don't have to make it all happen. You just have to take one step forward, in faith, and let Him do the rest. Where you can't, God already has."[4]

"And let us run with perseverance the race marked out for us, fixing our eyes on Jesus, the pioneer and perfecter of faith" (Hebrews 12:1–2).

When I first became a mom, I bought in to the lie that I was enough on my own. I even purchased all kinds of kitschy affirmation wall art materials to remind me of that. Even though there is no social media evidence of this because #PinterestFail, I promise you I made a valiant effort with sticky notes and magic markers. And each time I failed, it was even more soul crushing than the time before, because I was supposed to be a rock star. I was enough, people! I've got this! Well, I can't tell you how many times I've dialed my mom at 3:00 a.m. to tearfully admit, "I *can't* do this!" Now, sadly, she doesn't even pick up the phone when I call (apparently, some people have to sleep or something), but God is *always* there. He's always there to talk it out. Even at 3:00 a.m.

Oh, how I wish I had known then what I have learned now. What a burden-lifter to realize that Christ is our "enough"! I want to generate a new quote image that reads: "We are enough *in* Christ!"

If we rely on our earthly wants like sleep, peace, quiet, and the list goes on, we are missing out on all the beauty found in relying solely on God's grace and His promise to carry us in *all* circumstances. It's so easy to say, "I can't do this!" What if instead we exclaimed, "Look what Christ can do *through* me!" (Philippians 4:13; Jeremiah 17:7)? Leaning on Christ is *not* a sign of weakness. It is a visible reminder of the strength we gain from relying on His direction. "True confidence is really 'God-confidence.' It's not so much about believing in ourselves as it is about believing in what God can do through us."[5] Let's give up on our quest of being Mommy of the Year and instead fall into the arms of our super-powered God. "But he said to me, my grace is sufficient for you, for my power is made perfect in weakness" (2 Corinthians 12:9).

"It's only when we acknowledge who we really are *apart* from Christ—sinful, broken, prone to wander—that we will live in gratitude for who we are *in* Christ—beloved, chosen, and beautiful before our holy God."[6] God chose a simple man, who to the world was nothing but a carpenter, and saved the entire world from sin—the single greatest gift of all time. So why then can't we imagine that He would use regular moms like me and you, even on our *worst* days, to raise up our children for His kingdom?

Friend, you are more than enough in Christ. A whole lotta 'nuff. All. The. 'Nuff. And with Christ as your guide, you can do anything through Him who gives you strength. Jesus paid it all for you at Calvary. But He gives us more grace. That is why Scripture says, "God opposes the proud but shows favor to the humble" (James 4:6). He nailed all your late-night gossip sessions, ruined dinners, tardy attendance, sloppy getups, cussing fits, and messy rooms right there on the cross. And that's where you can leave them too.

6

Ghosting on the Guilt Goblins

Baby registries are so cool. Who doesn't love going to the store, using one of those super-fun pricing guns, and clicking everything in there like it's raining hundred-dollar bills? Anyone remember the TV show *Supermarket Sweep*? Well, if not, google it and enjoy an afternoon of sheer delight. Those contestants depict the contagious joy that would most certainly be felt by running through a baby store with reckless abandon, screaming Oprah-style, "You get a Baby Bjorn! And you get an UPPAbaby stroller! And you get [insert your own version of super-sought-after, over-priced baby item here]!" But I think we are extending our registries outside the big-box baby stores and on to parenting these days. And that's *not* so cool.

When we begin this parenting journey, it's natural for us to reach out for help/advice for surviving this season. Then it becomes tempting to throw all those different tips on parenting into our baskets of baby-raising, and we start to feel overwhelmed. Just when we thought we'd finally checked the box of feeling like we are enough, and we might even be getting pretty good at this whole motherhood thing, the big bad goblin of guilt comes in and sets up camp. We start worrying about things like getting back on our career path after maternity leave, or traveling during the week when society says we should be at home with our family, or sending our kids to *that* school instead of the school all the other kids are attending, or does my butt look good in these mom jeans?

It occurred to me that we are all circulating between one or more types of mom guilt on a daily basis:

1. "Coulda, Woulda, Shoulda" Guilt—this is that pit in your stomach that is constantly lying to you, saying you made some kind of "wrong" decision. Maybe you *could've* tried longer at breastfeeding, maybe you *should've* gone back to work, or maybe you *would've* gone natural on the birthing table if that first contraction hadn't felt like the beginning of the end of the world as you knew it.

2. "Can I Just" Guilt—this is that emotion that washes over you when all you can think is, *Can I just go out and enjoy one night with my girlfriends without my kids reminding me for twenty-five consecutive days that Mommy was, in fact, not home to brush teeth on Tuesday, March the 28th, in the year of our Lord 2018, as the reason they are entitled to seventeen more bags of fruit snacks?*

3. "Can't Do It" Guilt—this is the extra-bad guy who shows up at 3:00 a.m., when you're in your feelings about everything, and no pint of Ben & Jerry's is gonna make it any better. Thank the good Lord, His compassions come new every morning. "Because of the LORD's great love we are not consumed, for his compassions never fail. They are new every morning; great is your faithfulness. I say to myself, 'The LORD is my portion; therefore I will wait for him'" (Lamentations 3:22–24).

"Therefore I will wait for him." Did y'all see that in the verse above too? Sometimes I sit around waiting on *Him* for a while because I just don't have a clue what to do. "God created us to *thrive* in the unwavering assurance of His love, which is given to us because of

Jesus. But, instead of thriving in God's love, most of us are doing something radically different. We are *striving*. Striving for something that is actually already ours."[7]

Let me ask you a friendly question about parenting today, may I? Do you have this whole parenting thing all figured out? Do you know what to do in *every* possible situation? If you do, I would like to personally invite you to email me at the address I will provide at the end of this book, and I will connect you to the right people, because we need to get that word out, sister. But, if like me, you feel at times that you have no clue what the heck to do in any given situation, much less how to manage fitting in a shower over the course of seven days, then I submit that this chapter was written specifically for you.

Heads up: We are going to be pitched and teased the "newest invention/discovery in motherhood" every day for the rest of our lives, and they will all seem groundbreaking, lifesaving, and truly revolutionary—at first. Then, after a few weeks, the newness of these parenting plans wear off, and we are stuck with whatever we have going on with Christ.

Well, let's ask ourselves, have we prayed about it? Have we asked God what *He* wants us to do? This may not be front-page news, but last I checked, all the mom bloggers, your nosy neighbor next door, and yes, even Oprah, are *not* the ones tasked with determining whether or not you are a "good mom." I want to humble myself on my mom journey by asking for help, since I know I cannot manage it all. I want to be courageous enough to push through the hard days. And I want to remind myself to be grateful to God for His never-ending grace in all situations.

So I propose a renewed parenting plan.

Jesus.

All the time, Jesus.

We've got to get a whole lot of "God-fidence" going on up in here! This renewed Christ-focused parenting is the real deal because there are *no* other perfect parenting plans. Hallelujah!

We don't even need to worry about all the other styles of parenting out there. There are way too many now anyway: crunchy, vegan, scrunchy, organic, baby-wearing, "normal"—I mean who can even keep up?! And, if there really was one perfect style of parenting, don't you think God in His infinite awesomeness would have included an addendum at the end of Revelation that said, "Oh yeah, and for all you mommas, check out ~~Girlfriend's~~ God's Guide to Parenting, available wherever books are sold!"

What if all the women in the Bible had been identical in every way? We would have learned nothing from them. We wouldn't have Martha to teach us to sit down and appreciate the season. Eve would have never taught us that sin can present itself in many different forms. We wouldn't have had Hannah to teach us that even in our darkest seasons of waiting, God is with us always. Think with me for a moment. If we were all the same, why would God have created the infinitely differing options we have to exercise in our parenting?

I choose to avoid the label maker and rest in the truth that the key to motherhood is found within each of our hearts and in the only manual we ever really need—God's Word—which means all our parenting "styles" are going to be different. God will provide each of us the best tools, the best plans, and the best instructions for how to nurture our little ones, if only we seek His direction. "Do not conform to the pattern of this world, but be transformed by the renewing of your mind. Then you will be able to test and approve what God's will is—his good, pleasing and perfect will" (Romans 12:2).

God will provide us all the answers we could ever dream up and will afford us the strength when we need it most. If we give God our weaknesses, He will give us His strength. After all, God is in control. He is all-knowing, all-powerful, and wise. Don't take it from me, just ask Him. "Even youths grow tired and weary, and young men stumble and fall; but those who hope in the LORD will renew their strength. They will soar on wings like eagles; they will run and not grow weary, they will walk and not be faint" (Isaiah 40:30–31).

....

God will provide each of us the best tools, the best plans, and the best instructions for how to nurture our little ones, if only we seek His direction.

....

So when we find ourselves fretting over the next mommy-doubt issue, let's scream out to God (Pro Tip: No literal screams if baby(ies) are sleeping) and ask Him to give us guidance and peace. Let's ask *Him* to grant us the wisdom necessary to make the best decisions for our little ones.

I'm going to drop a few truths that God has, ever-so-gently, breathed into my heart when I was lying on the floor, crying out to Him a bajillion times before. Wisdom comes from God. We don't ever need to boast of our ability, but rather of God's strength through us. In all situations, He is ready and able to guide us along our journeys, even catching us when we fall. "If any of you lacks wisdom [insert all mothers umpteen times throughout the day], you should ask God, who gives generously to all [praise Jesus!] without finding fault [so undeserving], and it will be given to you [better than Christmas morning, y'all]" (James 1:5).

Finally, in life, especially along the parenting journey, make *this* your fight song: "Trust in the LORD with all your heart and lean not on your own understanding; in all your ways submit to Him, and He will make your paths straight" (Proverbs 3:5–6).

7

Botox Bingo
or Bible Study Brunch?

When I was a little girl, my dad often drove us to school. Looking back, I think those fifteen minutes in the car each day have become some of his favorite moments in life. He loved to sing loudly, scare us by abruptly screaming out at stop signs, and wave to random people as we sped by them. He also found embarrassing us in the carpool line a daily requirement (still does, for that matter).

Sunglasses with giant royal-blue rims were his accessory of choice for the endeavor. He would wait until we were *just* about to unload and throw those hideously gigantic shades on his face to greet our friends. As our teachers and classmates would point and laugh, I will never forget what he would say: "What kind of day are we going to have?" He would wait until we responded (though oftentimes we declined), then, as if out of nowhere, he would scream, "*Great day!*" No matter what kind of mood I was in, that one daily dialogue always (secretly) brought a smile to my face.

A few weeks ago, I needed my dad to remind me of the importance of frame of mind. The rain was coming down in thick sheets as we traveled down the road. I had already burned the waffles that morning, and slipped and fell down the stairs to the garage, my Bio-Oil wasn't working on those stubborn stretch marks, and now my older daughter needed to "go potty" fifteen minutes away from our destination. I was ready to call it a day, crawl back in bed, and hide under the covers. As we crested a hill, I noticed a quaint little chapel nestled among some tall pines. At the edge of the parking lot was a sign that read "Every day will not be great. But there will be something GREAT about every day."

Wow. God shows up, doesn't He? Right when we reach the brink of desperation, He's there, reaching a hand out to catch us from a fall.

I started to think about the message from the sign that day, and my heart realized God was posturing me for an attitude adjustment, just like my dad had done for me every day as a child. When we go through the motions each day, it's so easy to get worn down, beat up, and exhausted, and just never feel like enough. It's completely understandable. Things are not always perfect—*they can't be*! We might even find ourselves leaning toward a Negative Nancy mentality at times, but if we take a moment each morning before our feet even hit the floor to say, "Today is going to be a great day. I have the gift of another day. Let's do this!" we have already started our day off on a positive note.

So often in life, attitude and perspective are everything. Full disclosure: The fact that you woke up and continue to exist may be the *only* "great" parts of some days. Don't let that discourage you. If you look at life through a positive lens (take, for example, giant royal-blue-rimmed sunglasses), you are destined to see the good in your reality rather than focusing on the bad.

One of the first things that happens, once we become parents, is the "You Are Not Good Enough" Thief comes to town (aka satan), and he points out everything that could ever possibly be "wrong": our thighs are thicker, the baby isn't getting enough milk, our homes are literal wrecks on the highway where only trolls could reside peacefully within, our precious in-laws (insert whomever lovingly drives you to the brink of insanity here) have crafted forty-seven new reasons why we just aren't making the cut, and we don't know what to do.

At this point, if you are anything like me, you descend into a silent depression of insecurity and unworthiness. You question all your choices and stay up at night, ironically, for reasons other than a crying infant. "Insecurity is bondage to who we're not. Confidence is freedom in who we are!"[8] Well, let's attack those personal triggers of insecurity and unworthiness first. If we are honest, those often hurt the worst because they feel like areas in which *we* have managed to fail *ourselves*.

All of us have blemishes now because of our journeys. We may dress differently, look differently, act differently, and think differently, but at the end of the day, we mommas have all been changed for the better.

Allow me to share with you my new philosophy when the enemy comes for this momma. We've talked about what our kids think about perfection. Now let's talk about what *God* thinks.

God is *not* concerned about the size of our thighs, the status of our laundry rooms, or the condition of our midsections. He is concerned with the condition of our *hearts*—cue a "Hallelujah Chorus," followed closely by an old-school Southern-Baptist-style rendition of "What a Mighty God We Serve."

Rather than lining up for Botox Bingo, maybe we should check into a little Bible Study Brunch, because, after all, the superficial fixes we seek on this earth pale in comparison to the heavenly change we can find in Him.

The *world* loves us for our perfections, but *God* celebrates our imperfections—the things He so carefully crafted to make us unique in our own ways.

The *world* loves us as our bodies get smaller, but *God* loves us regardless of our body size. Rather, He rejoices the bigger our hearts get.

It's vital for us to accept ourselves exactly as God has designed us—both before and *after* baby. We want to point our children to a God who *never* makes mistakes and creates us all beautiful, in His own image. God is in the business of using imperfect people to live out His perfect plan—booty dimples and all, friends!

I love 2 Corinthians 5:17: "Therefore, if anyone is in Christ, the new creation has come: The old has gone, the new is here!" I have to confess that even though I may be playing it fast and loose with the *true* biblical meaning of this verse, I like to apply this to my new mom-bod and #MomLife by adjusting the words just a bit: "Therefore, if any of you is a momma, a new life (and body) have come! The old has gone, the new is here!"

Take a look at what I mean.

These bags under our eyes represent the hours we spend nurturing our little ones. We could be enjoying blissful sleep with no distractions, but we are called to something so much greater. Our babies need grace and love, *just like we do*. And these bags, while temporary, are permanent reminders that a little lack of sleep is certainly worth the love we share with our God-given gifts.

These stretch marks remind us that we have been gifted the new title of "Mom." We were able to carry our babies on our own. God chose to use *our* bodies as the vessels to bring our little ones into this world. And He just so happened to leave a special reminder of those moments. They are unsightly and even scary (I feel this so hard), but, rather than scoffing at their presence, we will thank Him for blessing us with our family.

This cellulite on our thighs seemed to pack on fast after baby number one. We can all agree that we were appalled at its emergence, but we can choose to look at it as a constant reminder that we *all* have areas of improvement. We can thank God for the opportunity to explore those improvements. Our bodies are temples, and even the grandest of temples have blemishes.

This pain in our backs has resulted from years of lifting, carrying, and chasing little ones. We could sit and complain about it, or we could take a Tylenol and remind ourselves that there will come a day when we will wish we could chase them around at home, rather than at the mall or at some friend's house nearby.

These missed calls from friends are reminders that our priorities have drastically changed—for the better. Rather than spending our time appeasing our own desires, we are reveling in the opportunity to create our newest little #Squad.

These shrinking bank accounts are *super* stressful. These stacks of bills make us want to crawl into a hole and hide, but snuggling at home is way better than keepin' up with the Joneses any day. Ramen noodles never tasted better since they come coupled with a big bear hug. And the smiles on those innocent, grateful faces make every penny—and lack thereof—worthwhile.

These trashed cars look like city dumpsters. You would think we are raising twenty-seven children with all the trash collecting going on up in here. But those crackers crushed into the carpet means somebody was fed that day. The crayons melting into the seats means someone found joy in coloring, and the ballet shoes strewn about in the backseat means someone is on a fun adventure. Today we will be grateful to even have a vehicle to transport these little ones on their journeys of life.

These laundry rooms full of dirty, nasty, stinky clothes are over-whelming, quite honestly. We avoid them at all costs most days, but today we are going to gaze at the tiny clothes and think about the little bodies who wear them—the little bodies that danced into our lives and changed us (and our laundry rooms) for the better.

These dens are full of junk. Our guests must think we have been collecting for a gigantic charitable donation for months. (Wait, *guests*? What are those? There's been a "Quarantined" sign on our homes for years.) But that's really okay. We don't have time to don our aprons right now anyway. Instead, we can pause to reminisce about all the fun moments we share here, and plan for hundreds more.

> You are beautiful. You are strong. And you are more
> than enough in Christ!

These increasingly sloppy getups we've got going on are probably not appealing to those forced to view them, but to our babies, these PJs mean Mommy is ready to be jumped on, snuggled with, kissed, and wrestled on the floor. They mean we've got all the time in the world to do some lovin'.

Whew. That's a whole lotta little merry sunshine, but sometimes it's important to kick ole Negative Nancy out the door (no offense to any of you precious readers named Nancy. Y'all rock and give Nancy a good name) and remind yourself that it's all about perspective and choosing gratitude. Maybe even throw on a pair of giant blue sunglasses if you need a little extra nudge of happy.

I hope whenever you get down or compare yourself to others, as we *all* will from time to time, you will always remember that these earthly blemishes, stresses, and changes are actually heavenly reminders of God's infinite grace.

You are beautiful. You are strong. And you are more than enough in Christ!

"Rejoice always, pray continually, give thanks in all circumstances; for this is God's will for you in Christ Jesus" (1 Thessalonians 5:16–18).

CHEERS TO ...

- ♨ Being confident in the fact that you are enough just the way you are in Christ.
- ♨ Releasing yourself of the pressures of the Boss Babe/Super Mom mentality.
- ♨ Accepting your so-called flaws as reminders of the strength and abilities God blessed you with when He named you "Mom."

- Knowing that you do not have to be the hero and you can't do it all—but God can.
- Equipping yourself with the truth that Christ is your enough, so you can rest in His grace in all situations.
  - You are going to feel "not enough" in life (Romans 8:23).
  - But God's Word doesn't leave you parked in that hopelessness (1 Peter 2:9).
  - On those days when the "Enough" Thief comes to town, remember this: "For I am convinced that neither death nor life, neither angels nor demons, neither the present nor the future, nor any powers, neither height nor depth, [neither epic fails nor mommy mayhem, nor stretch marks, nor thunder thighs], nor anything else in all creation, will be able to separate us from the love of God that is in Christ Jesus our Lord" (Romans 8:38–39).
- Today's Celebration: Decide today to stop chasing after unrealistic enough-ness. Find hope in the fact that you don't have to have it all figured out, you don't have to be an expert on potty training, you don't have to know the meaning and solution every time your baby cries, and you certainly don't have to have your child's life planned out for the next eighteen years. Put up that new Instagram graphic, girl: *You are enough in Christ!*

Free yourself of the expectations that you may not even realize you have placed on yourself. I want you to do so, but, more importantly, God's Word tells you to do so. You are enough just the way you are—in Christ who has set you free!

You Are Not Alone

Mom Confession: Even though I have toddlers clinging to my ankles, *VeggieTales* blasting in the background, and what seems like a never-ending text message chain with my Mommy-and-Me-Zumba buds, this mommy thing feels isolating and, dare I say, lonely at times.

CHEERS TO ...

TRUTH #3 – You Always Have Support in Christ and in Your Tribe (Even at 2:00 a.m.)

Christ is your solace in the tough and in the lonely. Cultivating your mom tribe and digging into the Word will leave you full of love and the hope that you are, in fact, never alone, even on the toughest of days.

....

"Have I not commanded you? Be strong and courageous. Do not be afraid; do not be discouraged, for the LORD your God will be with you wherever you go."

JOSHUA 1:9

8

Is Anybody Out There?

Not even twenty minutes after I delivered my first baby, my family began asking me what I would like for dinner. I had been tickled with excitement surrounding my first post-pregnancy meal since day one and had planned it out with the diligence of a mother carrying a scanner at the local big-box department store, completing her baby registry. I promptly requested the two things all dreams are made of: a chili cheese dog and an ice-cold beer.

If you know me, you know that the chili cheese dog is a pretty standard request from yours truly, but the beer came completely out of left field. After my dream meal arrived, I sat in the glider with my baby girl and stared into her gorgeous eyes. She was (and is) perfect. She cooed and I ahhed. She dribbled slobber on her chin as I devoured my chili cheese dog—a girl after my own heart.

But as we were sitting there, I quickly discovered something else that came out of left field: *loneliness*. All my family members had retreated to checking things off the now full-to-the-brim to-do list, and it was just the two of us. It was eerily silent, and the thought of this type of solitude was suddenly paralyzing.

Mommyhood consists of dream-glider moments and squishy toddler perma-hugs fueled by steroid-laced Cheerios. But you know what else it can be? *Lonely.* Sometimes even outright scary. Anytime I say that to someone, they look at me like I'm crazy. How could you possibly be lonely when you are surrounded by two vivacious toddlers day in and day out?

As much as I am thrilled to spend all my waking hours snuggling, kissing, and squeezing these bundles of joy till their heads pop off, it turns out that they don't seem to care about much other than Barbies and tea parties. And while that's completely normal, it can leave Momma at a loss for more mature interactions and necessary adult bonds.

Our little tots are often not familiar with the world's current events, and any conversation topic other than "What treat am I getting if I eat all my green beans tonight?" is too taxing for their tiny attention spans. Plus, word on the street informs me that babies have no appreciation for mimosa brunches either.

In an effort to spell out my solidarity to you, sister, I want to enlighten you on a few things:

The days are going to be long, and exhausting, and challenging. *You are not alone.*

The hairs on the back of your neck are going to stand up when your baby pukes for the first time. *You are not alone.*

The fact that you now know all the characters on Paw Patrol and find yourself debating what Marshall would do in any given moment is going to make you feel like a complete basket case. *You are not alone.*

The fear that you are not up to the constant challenges of parenting, causing you to feel like checking yourself in to a recurring therapy session (or twelve), will creep in—often more than once throughout the day. *You are not alone.*

The frustration of wolfing down a few handfuls of goldfish crackers as your "lunch" for the forty-seventh day in a row will make you feel like a vagabond. *You are not alone.*

The feeling that no one sees you, no one hears you, and no one understands you will pervade your thoughts. At the same time, the feeling that you can't find a quiet place and you haven't heard a thought in your own head for months, and the fear of something (or someone) even grazing your thigh will make you sweat in the worst of anxiety-filled ways. *You are not alone.*

The overwhelming urge to cram yourself in the cabinet under your sink, not so much as a killer Hide-and-Seek spot but more so as a survival-of-the-fittest tactic, will pop up on the daily. *You are not alone.*

Checking the front door for your whipping boy (I mean husband) to swoop in and save the day, beginning at around 3:30 p.m. every afternoon, is going to make you feel like a jerk/world-renowned conqueror of excellence all at the same time. The shock, coupled with elation that you and the kids survived another day, will be intoxicating. *You are not alone.*

The rush of hormone-laced emotions is going to ravage your soul at the most inopportune times. *You are not alone.*

The sun will rise, even after a day when you thought there was no hope for a better tomorrow. *You are not alone.*

If you don't read anything else in this whole book, I want you to read and repeat this to yourself daily: *I. Am. Not. Alone.*

I wish more mothers would be honest about this feeling of no-man's-land that exists after bringing our babies home from the hospital. It's a real thing, and we all experience it. Don't feel guilty about it, but don't ignore it either. Sometimes it's best to lean in to it and discover ways to combat it.

Which leads us to the handy-dandy, tried-and-true plan for helping kick those lonely feelings right on out to the curb ...

9

The Ultimate Guide to Tappin' Your Momma Tribe

alluded to this earlier, but back in 2012, I started dating again—and not my hubby. If you are doing the math, *yes*, I was married at the time. And this new dating game has been the hottest, most life-affirming dating process of my life—with the exception of that season with said hubby, of course.

I'm talking about tappin' my tribe, y'all.

As mommas, we need a select group of people surrounding us to make this life everything it's meant to be and more. Because, as precious as our little ones are, they are *not* created to fulfill us—only God can do that.

But here on this earth, we need companionship. "We were meant to do life together. We were created for community. There is a new friend out there who needs you just as much as you need her."[9] "A friend loves at all times" (Proverbs 17:17), "Therefore encourage one another and build each other up, just as you are doing" (1 Thessalonians 5:11).

We need wise counsel: "Listen to advice and accept discipline, and at the end you will be counted among the wise" (Proverbs 19:20).

And sometimes we just need somebody to make us laugh: "He

will yet fill your mouth with laughter and your lips with shouts of joy" (Job 8:21).

At the end of the day, we all need to vent about this crazy, beautiful stage of life we're in. I wish there was a Mommy Rant Wall (maybe I'll create it) where we could flock to some virtual location and anonymously share our triumphs *and* woes of the day. Sort of a judgment-free venting zone. *Sounds amazing, right?* The kind of place that offers no shame when you deliver the news that your child had a complete meltdown at the grocery store, really showing off her threenager skills by yelling at the kind employee who swiftly bagged your purchases to avoid any contact whatsoever with your tiny terror.

Seventy-five calls to our own mommas each day lamenting about our most-recent struggles often just doesn't do the trick. After the "Well, I told you this is what it would be like," and the "Oh, [insert child's name here] is a saint; she could never act like that," retorts from dear old Mom, we realize the need for a kindred group of women fighting the good fight together.

True story: I once bonded with one of my new besties after simply exchanging photos of our dumpster-fire-level closets. Like, not even the Instagram-famous home organizers The Home Edit (or whomever you would trust to accept the challenge of organizing your life) would have taken on our disasters. That girl is now a sister to me. All it took was someone being vulnerable, open, real, and *honest*.

All we really need is a sounding board who will sit quietly while we vent. Someone who will expose their areas of shame so that we can feel free to open up about our own. Someone who will wipe *our* tears, hold *our* hands, and kiss *our* cheeks.

It's okay to admit we need help. It's perfectly fine for us to cling to our support system. In fact, it's necessary. We do need our moms. We need willing neighbors to lend a hand and an uplifting smile. We need friends who will have our backs rather than judge our journeys. We need love, not hate. More than anything, we *need* Jesus Christ holding our hands every step of the way. "For where two or three gather in my name, there am I with them" (Matthew 18:20).

So, what do we do about this? *We tap our tribe.* Have you ever heard the phrase "Your vibe attracts your tribe?" Well, get your vibe mojo up and running, girl, and go tap yo tribe! Tap 'em everywhere! Imagine me in waiting rooms of ballet studios, the carpool line at school, and aisles at the grocery store just stalking my hopefully new-bestie prey. Speed-date at church, in Bible study, or at the mall. Select a few girls who make you feel good and create your sisterhood. That's how it's done.

Tapping a tribe is *not* a simple task and it will take time, but let me promise you right now that it is worth *all* the effort. I'm even going to go out on a limb here and proclaim it to be one of the most important things you will do during motherhood, outside of parenting your babes.

I've put together a list of what my tribe looks like in hopes that you might be inspired to find yours. Disclaimer: Please do *not* feel overwhelmed by this list, friend. I have just included my ideal tribe when life feels somewhat perfect and I am killin' the friendship game. But I will say, I am constantly on the hunt for any of these individuals who I may be missing at any given time. Feel free to pick your favorite two to start with, and you can "collect" the others as you go.

The Adulting Aficionado

This woman makes Martha Stewart look like a DIY-attempting fool. She's got it *all* together. She can whip up a divine four-course dinner in stilettos and still deliver the most incredible story-time session you've ever observed twenty minutes later at bedtime. Her knowledge is offensively vast, and her stamina is shame-inducing. It's like she sweats diamonds, for heaven's sake. Just call her "Life's Cruise Director."

She knows the exact pediatric-approved bathwater temperature and the cleanest hands-on children's museum, but she can also direct you to the most delicious sangria in town. Ladies, when you discover this woman, mooch off her brain like there's no tomorrow. She will save you hundreds of dollars in self-help parenting books and late-night Google sessions.

The Epic-Fail Enthusiast

There's no other way to describe this addition to our momma tribe arsenal than referring to her as the epitome of epic fails—aka the antithesis of the Adulting Aficionado. Her photo is the descriptive image accompanying the term *disheveled* in the dictionary.

She's a pro at ~~dropping children off balconies~~ salvaging toddler tumbles and sporting two-month-old pancake stains on her off-the-shoulder workout tank. Her hair tied up in a topknot isn't as much fashionable as it is functional—and necessary—considering she's been rocking dry-shampooed locks for the last ~~month~~ week and a half (if we're being generous). She may be the most genuine member of your tribe because she is eternally unbothered by anything other than raw authenticity, no matter how helter-skelter that may be.

The free-to-be-me mentality is never more wholeheartedly embraced than by the Epic-Fail Enthusiast. God love her soul, she is everything we never knew we needed because she is the reminder that no matter how bad we think we've got it, somebody else is trudging along an even-more-harried terrain.

The Carefree Crusader

This lady, by definition, is that tried-and-true single friend. It's incredibly refreshing to engage in conversation with her because she is *not* emotionally invested in Princess Sophia or The Berenstain Bears' latest adventures. In fact, she's probably never even heard of either of them. Maybe you've known her for ages, or maybe you recently just met. Nevertheless, she is the one you run to when you wish to live vicariously (if only for a moment) in the land of single-dom. Once she's made you acutely aware of the many land grenades lurking in the world that is single life, you breathe in a euphoric sigh of relief, realizing that in so many ways maybe you really *do* have life all figured out.

While all the single ladies put their hands up (I see you, Beyoncé, I'm pickin' up what you're puttin' down) and delve off into the bone-crushing world of online dating/set-ups/breakups/emotional beatdowns and frustration, we members of the momma tribe will feel just fine lying down on the couch, putting on our night masks, and cascading into (albeit interrupted—and desperately needed) sleep.

The Eternal Encourager

God. Bless. This. Precious. Soul. It seems her perma-grin must be the result of years of plastic surgery. But *no*, she is simply one of God's special gifts. She always has an uplifting word and/or friendly hug. The warmth of her soul radiates from feet away, soothing you like a mug of hot chocolate on a cold winter's night. When I think of an Eternal Encourager, I envision a verbal Twitter feed of scrolling motivational quotes. Adding her to your tribe ensures that no matter what, you will never forget that there *is* still good in this world.

The Playdate-Planning Princess

I rarely get my grocery list in order, much less have the time to think up, plan, and execute the oh-so-necessary playdate. Enter the Playdate-Planning Princess. This momma, like you, is longing for a lady to add to her tribe who needs a day out of the house with her kids once in a while. She's organized. She's friendly. She's awesome. You can spot her from a mile away, as she's the precious one who breaks the ice in the ballet studio waiting room. Love her. Embrace her. She is your ticket to sanity next Tuesday at 10:00 a.m.

The Same-Stage Survivor

Has there ever been a deeper kindred spirit on this earth than a fellow mom walking through the *exact* same stage you are? Answer, no. Nope. No ma'am. This individual has been gifted to you directly from God to pick you up off the bathroom floor when you think you are the *only* mother in America cleaning barf off crib rails at 3:32 a.m. She's the *only* one who understands the comfort (both physically and psychologically) that yoga pants provide, and, most likely, the *only* human therapist who can prevent you from tending to that longstanding desire to imbibe in those emergency bottles of wine.

The Step-Ahead Sorcerer

This woman does not pretend to be a walking encyclopedia, but she sure does have a catalog of invaluable *experience*-laced magic crammed in her brain. She's walked the weary roads, wiped the tears, and learned the tough lessons—you know, the ones we all so desperately wish to avoid learning ourselves. She can walk you through the next step in the valley before you even arrive at that upcoming mountain. The Step-Ahead Sorcerer is key for avoiding regret and the "I wish I had known" feelings. She's been there, so you don't have to.

The Party-Bus Phenom

Ladies night! Mommas, how many times a week do you stare out your front window, watching the cars pass by around 6:00 p.m., and think, *Bet they're going to an Italian restaurant to feed on decadent pasta, followed by a super-fun dance session at the local bar?* Just me? Oh …

Sometimes we are in a seemingly life-or-death need for a night out. To dust off the fun wardrobe, finally fix our hair, and take the world by storm. To chat about margarita flavors rather than breast-milk storage-bag providers—ugh! And, you know, so we can finally contribute to those jealousy-inducing Instagram pics for a change.

Well, with the Party-Bus Phenom in your momma tribe, you will never have to lust after random strangers and their cool agendas ever again.

The Bible-Beating Belle

Jesus takes her wheel non-stop. So this homegirl is available to help when you need somebody to take yours too. She's got the exact Bible verse you need for every occasion in life and can spout it off without even thinking. In fact, she may even have affirmation cards showcasing handwritten calligraphy in her purse, if you need some on-demand inspiration from the Word. She's constantly organizing the next Bible study, and you know that list can get more exclusive than the Oscars' red carpet, so you definitely want to stay on her good side.

The Lifer

This girl was lying in the bassinet beside you when you came home from the hospital. Okay, maybe not, but it sure feels that way. She's been with you through thick and thin, and she has no plans of quitting you, Momma! It doesn't matter what stage of life you are in, what country you reside in, or what is on the agenda, the two of you would move heaven and earth to be there for one another—the Thelma to your Louise.

She knows all your secrets and loves you just the same. She was there for you during your ugly-duckling-awkward middle-school stage, and she'll be there for you as you browse for fifty-year wedding anniversary party venues. Cling to this woman like there is no tomorrow. There's nothing better than the evergreen, unwavering, unconditional bond of a Lifer.

Your Ride-or-Die Chick

This girl is ready to ride and isn't even bothered to inquire about the dying part. There's no time for silly questions like that, because she's too busy defending your parenting skills in the preschool hallway after Polly Preschool's momma informed everyone that your child had just finished a rousing no-pants dance during music class. She's also the mom who saved your kid from a horrific tumble at the playground last week when you stepped away for 0.0002 seconds to discard the slobbery popsicle stick he almost shoved down his throat while haphazardly hanging from the monkey bars. This girl will begin to feel more like a soldier in your army rather than simply your best friend, and that's when you'll know you need to upgrade her status to Ride-or-Die.

Late-night shame-inducing fast-food run? *She's there.*

Binge-watching your favorite TV show, even though she despises the main character? *She's there.* No big deal. In fact, she'll be there with bells on while chomping away on a bucket of popcorn, taking mental notes for discussion later.

And, most importantly, when you call her at 4:52 a.m. to inform her that you *finally* chunked the breast pump out the second-story window and prayed a stray dog would drag it to the city dump, *she'll be there.* She will never judge you and will likely share a story about how she stubbed her kid's toe somewhat on purpose earlier in the day.

This girl is your sister from another mister. Love her. Hold on to her like she's the last hot toy in Target at Christmastime and you've gotta make it to the checkout line before everybody else. She is your soul's counterpoint in another.

Your Own Momma

There are days when the *only* thing that gets me through is a fifteen-second chat with my momma. *And everyone said, "Amen."* This woman birthed you and raised you, and now she's holding your hand down your own crazy journey of motherhood. Every woman has a very different relationship with their momma, but I think we can all agree on one thing: there's no replacement for a mother-daughter connection. There's an ESP present in those relationships that doesn't exist elsewhere. I'm betting it has to do with the ten months we spent surviving off her very existence—just sayin'.

Christ

I saved the best for last. We can have all the tribe sisters in the world, but if we don't have Christ, we will still always feel empty. He is the only One who will always be by our side, always be our confidant, and always have the answers we so desperately need.

I undervalued the power of prayer until I found myself in a 24/7 state of prayer—you feel me? Phrases like "Jesus, take the wheel," "God, help me," and "Fix it, Jesus!" are *not* slang phrases in my household. They are fervent, intentional cries out to the only One who can help me in my frequent states of need.

True story: One of my older child's first spoken phrases was an empowered scream of "Jesus, take it!" Too often, we forget to reach out and lean on God. He happens to be available whenever we need Him. His schedule is never too busy. His phone lines are never tied up. He even works on nights and weekends, people! It's so tempting to search for the missing piece to our puzzles in our husband, our Ride-or-Die Chick, or even our babies, but we will always feel unfulfilled until we learn to depend solely on Him. So, when tappin' your tribe, don't forget to add the most important One to your list!

CHEERS TO ...

- 🦆 Becoming besties. All the feels for you, girl.
- 🦆 Reminding yourself that you are not alone on this journey.
- 🦆 Finding friendship. Finding friends and learning how to be a good friend are necessary for thriving in mommyhood. If you would like more info about what the Bible says regarding being a good friend, I've tucked a handy-dandy list on my site, titled "The 15 F's of Friendship." If you get a chance, check it out and let it be your guide when tappin' your tribe!
- 🦆 Knowing that when you are facedown on the bathroom floor, thinking the world is most certainly coming to an

end, there's another momma there too. And you can take hope in the fact that God will pick you both back up and help you soar stronger than ever.

🦆 Today's Celebration: Think about all the places you socialize throughout the week—work, church, your child's Mother's Day Out or school program, exercise classes, grocery store, book clubs, Bible study, the hair salon, Target, etc. Make a list of the people you encounter on a weekly basis who you would like to get to know better. Spend this next week being very intentional about forming more personal relationships with those individuals. Text them. Call them. Invite them to lunch. Offer to take them dinner one night "just because." Sometimes all it takes is being the courageous one to make the first step to discover that a beautiful friendship existed all along!

PART IV

Conquering the Cray-Cray and Overcoming the Chaos of #MomLife

Mom Confession: Hi. There are moments during almost all my days when I could not for the life of me tell you where my sanity is located—because it certainly isn't present up in here.

CHEERS TO ...

TRUTH #4 – You Can Find Joy Even in the Craziness

Leaning (and sometimes literally falling) on Christ is your only chance at surviving this crazy, beautiful thing called parenting.

....

Yes, my soul, find rest in God; my hope comes from him.
Truly he is my rock and my salvation;
he is my fortress, I will not be shaken.

PSALM 62:5–6

10

Mamaste—Cultivating Calm Rather Than Chaos

Remember when parenting seemed peaceful and serene—you know, before we became parents ourselves? Right after college, when we pretended to be party planners and hosted baby showers for our friends as we oohed and ahhed over all the adorable baby gear. And what about all those commercials that depict motherhood as a never-ending Mommy and Me Yoga class—I'm guessing those advertising panels are staffed by men only?

So it seemed to us, leading into the journey, that parenting was predominantly "Twinkle, Twinkle Little Star," rather than "*Hush, Little Baby.*" Then, as the doctor yelled, "Push!" things suddenly got a whole lot more *namascray* rather than *namaste*.

Instead of meditating on yoga mats, we are thrust into the land of insanity and suddenly lose the ability to just *chill*. Breaking News Alert: There is no chill mode in parenting. Who's with me on this? I yell a whole lot more now than I ever have. (Unless you count my first year of law school, and it's frankly a blue wonder I survived that vortex of hellishness.)

I yell when I spill Rice Krispies all over the floor, or, God forbid, whenever I spilled even the tiniest amount of nature's golden nectar (also known as breastmilk) that I somehow managed to force out of my writing body. I yell when I step on those (insert non-Sunday-school-appropriate word here) screw tops to applesauce packs, which have somehow found their final resting places along the *exact* path I am planning to walk. And I yell when I unearth a sippy cup containing five-month-old curdled milk inside. Side Note: I talk about finding milk in sippy cups a lot. *Maybe I should see someone about this?* Admitting you have a problem is the first step in fixing it, right?

Well, I have come up with a new plan for all of us. You ready? This is how we are going to move forward whenever we feel the urge to have a total conniption fit.

Step 1: Place child(ren) in a safe location to ensure well-being for at least ten minutes.

Step 2: Promptly leave that area.

Step 3: Gather headphones and a snack—preferably chocolate.

Step 4: Locate a room within the house that has locking capabilities.

Step 5: Enter said room and lock the door immediately. Pro Tip: Do not forget this step.

Step 6: Pop open beverage, stick in headphones, crank up Flo Rida's "My House," and proceed to shake your groove thing like nobody's watching.

Step 7: Count to as many numbers as necessary to regain even an ounce of sanity. Pro Tip: Only re-engage with humanity once you are no longer seeing red.

I am, currently, curled up in my bed writing to you, taking one of these recommended "time-outs." I refer to my bed as my "safe place" because it is the only spot in my home that my children and I have come to an agreement about: when I retreat to this area, unless they have been extended an invitation to join me for popcorn and cuddle time or their head is literally on fire, momma needs a hot second.

You might have thought I would say that my bathroom is my safe place or, to be even more specific, my toilet, but as any mother will tell you, there are just some battles we will never win, folks.

Even so, there are still times we need solitude and the opportunity to vent about our cray-cray. We need to take "me" days and recharge. We need moments of solitude to re-center our focus and remind us of our blessings. We need to keep our massage therapist/nail stylist on speed dial. We need to declare one night a week "date night." As it turns out, babysitting services are much less expensive than divorce attorneys. Ponder on that.

We may even need to go to a room (padded or not), turn the lights off, and scream for as long as it takes to regain sanity. It's even okay to throw our hands in the air and wave 'em like we just don't care from time to time. There will be moments of desperation, and sometimes all we need to do is admit we *can't* do it all. Parents, much like children, need time-outs too.

Update: My safe place has been compromised because I just spilled an entire bottle of water everywhere, and I am having to strip the sheets like it's Saturday chore day. Ugh! Even our safe places are gonna let us down. The only *real* safe place we have from the chaos is not in two bottles of wine, not in a girls' weekend, and not even in our bedroom with multiple padlocks on the door. *It's in the arms of Christ!* That's it. That is the only tried-and-true safe haven we have.

....

It may not always be good with our circumstances, but it will always be good with our souls!

....

It would make me far less crazy if I could see God. Would it you? The truth is, He is always with us; sometimes we just have to look for Him.

He's in the tone of our children's voices when they exclaim their love for us.

He's the missing sock finally discovered wedged in the lint tray of the dryer.

He's the voice on the other end of the 8:00 p.m. phone call informing us that we *don't* have to drive carpool the next morning.

He's that tiny ray of sunshine that peeks out from a luminous cloud after a hard rain.

He's the green bean that our toddler finally decides to "try."

He's the kid-friendly "alarm clock" that gently reminds our kids *not* to bolt out of bed at 5:32 a.m. on Saturday mornings.

He's the craft our little one proudly waves at us with the words "I love you, Mommy!" scribbled all over it.

He's the sound of birds chirping outside, reminding us of the great big world we have inherited from Him.

We've got to stop looking at God as a coffee break and instead see Him as a constant lifeline (Deuteronomy 31:8)! It occurs to me that if we spent more time looking for our zen in God, rather than yoga studios, we might find He's been there all along.

When it's all said and done, mommyhood is not for wussies. These struggle buses aren't going to drive themselves, friends! We've already agreed that motherhood takes us straight down the highway to Crazytown, USA, but we *don't* have to camp out in the chaos. We can find our joy and cling to it, even if that joy is discovered in a five-minute somewhat-warm shower—*alone*—somewhere over there on Doing-the-Best-I-Can Drive. It may not always be good with our circumstances, but it will always be good with our souls!

So pat yourself on the back, friend. You are no wussy. You are a member of the momma tribe, and it's the greatest group of amazing women out there. This week let's all try to turn our namascray back into a little more "God is with us" *mamaste*.

11

Tasmanian Devils for Life!

Do you ever feel like no matter what you do, your house always looks like a bomb just went off, an intense burglary just occurred, and/or a tornado blew through? Because, yeah, kids = chaos. And it seems like no matter how hard we try to conquer the crazy, we end up like the Tasmanian Devil, furthering the definition of insanity!

It goes a little something like this:

Scenario 1

We proudly exclaim to the world (likely only the kitchen counter is listening) that we just finished loading the dishwasher. Kid in den thinks, *Great! I just destroyed the den. Good luck discovering the fermented waffle I just hid under the third sofa cushion!*

Scenario 2

We are just patting ourselves on the back for scrubbing that last bit of tile grout in the kids' shower when ... kid in playroom screams that she pooped her pants!

Scenario 3

Right as we are *about* to sit down (Ha! Let's get real, lean against a wall for a brief second) ... kid in kitchen dumps an entire box of Cheerios on the floor.

And all of those scenarios probably happened prior to 10:30 a.m. Ahh, mommyhood. Gotta love it!

It's a good thing I am not applying for a job at Merry Maids, because if a home visit was one of their requirements for employment, well, honey, there wouldn't be anything "merry" about it! The cleanliness aspect (I mean *un*cleanliness) of the parenting journey drives me crazy. Like pull-my-hair-out, need-a-sanity-break crazy. I'm admitting that to the world today because it's cathartic and it's honest.

But what if we started to see our messes as memories and our burdens as blessings? Think about this with me for a minute. Our crazy means we have children creating it—living, breathing blessings God has bestowed upon us. And while that is true and sounds great as we think about it, we still need some kind of solution, don't we?

If you think I'm going to provide you a list of the top five things to do to find your long-lost sanity, then we aren't tight enough yet, sister. Rather than giving you to-do lists of easily googled affirmation quotes or organizational strategies, I am going to tell you to embrace your Tasmanian Devil-ness and squeeze it till its head pops off. In that vein, I have a challenge to extend: If you can locate a mother who knows where her phone is at; whose children are fed, bathed, and in bed on time for a period of seven days straight; and who is simultaneously able to remain calm and never raise her voice, please introduce me to her. I commit to you today that I will release a second edition of this book with her sentiments on the matter. Spoiler Alert: You're never gonna find that looney tune!

What happens between our four walls can sometimes be fodder for a horror novel, or, in my case, ripe for an episode of *Hoarders* on HGTV. But if I think I'm the only one enduring this "craze phase," as I like to refer to it, I'm just kidding myself and keeping myself from experiencing that "You do that too?!" camaraderie with my fellow mommas.

So let's open up with each other today. I'll go first. How many of you are *also* members of the Wash the Load Three Times a Charm Laundry Club? You know what I mean. You throw a load in the washer. Insanity ensues. You return two days later, discover the old (now damp and smelly) load, and wash it again. Repeat previous steps. On the third day, you wash it again and stick Post-it notes everywhere to remind yourself to finally throw it in the dryer this time! I am a charter member of this club, actually. We voted last week to make me secretary (#HumbleBrag), although I'm not sure whether I should be honored or *embarrassed*.

I've always said that attempting to clean a house while raising children is like brushing your teeth while chomping on a mouthful of Oreos. It's just never gonna work. And while we are on this topic, can we chat for a minute about the whole "I'm so sorry my house is such a wreck!" game? Prior to company pop-ins (aka somewhat, kind-of uninvited guests), we spend forty-five minutes cramming toys into cubes, sweeping crumbs under china cabinets, and stuffing three loads of laundry into the dryer. We sweep, do the dishes, and wipe down the counter in a frantic craze to "get it together." Then we brush our hair back (or throw it up in the ever-popular mom bun, aka topknot), collect ourselves, and swing open the door, saying, "Come in! I am *so* sorry my house is such a wreck!"

Can I be honest? I am searching all over the world for that amazing woman out there who invites me over to her frat party-esque disaster of a house and doesn't even mention it. I desperately need to find the mom who will open the door to her home and invite me in *before* doing all that crazed cleaning—bonus points if she never even considered cleaning. I want to find my soul's counterpoint in another. I need a fellow hooligan who will stand up to this insanity and swing open the door to her circus like a deranged psychopath too. Because when a door is opened at one of my friend's homes and I am hit with the stench of Pine-Sol and a scented candle, I kinda want to punch them a little bit. I'm all like, "Where's your maid, girl!? Come out, come out, wherever you are!"

#RealTalk: My parents have had a Nerf gun bullet nastily stuck to the light fixture in their foyer for twelve years now. It has become the most endearing object in our family home, so long as you don't consider the sheer volume of my brother's saliva it required to permanently cement it there for over a decade. Mom and Dad have never even attempted to remove it. Wait. That's a lie. My dad gave up after considering the hefty insurance bill that would most assuredly accompany his rookie attempts of removing said Nerf gun bullet. So it is now affectionately referred to as our sentimental lighting "adornment." The truth is, we all have Nerf gun bullet moments, so let's celebrate them and revel in this crazy, awesome, non-*Southern Living* approved stage of life!

Friends, why do we care so much? Why are we so bothered by the thoughts of others? If these invitees are our friends, they ought to accept us regardless of whether or not we have pristine coasters on our side tables. Maybe, if we're lucky, we will locate our Ride-or-Die Chicks who are *also* playing it fast and loose with Emily Post's rules of domestication.

It points us to Galatians 1:10, doesn't it? Who are we really trying to please in life—God or man? We can't elevate the opinions of others above the intrinsic value and worth we have in Christ. When we notice ourselves caring more about what Susie Q says rather than bathing in God's grace, we've gotta check ourselves before we wreck ourselves.

We keep riding the hamster wheel of life, thinking that if we keep going, someone, hopefully God, will be proud. "But God doesn't want something *from* us. He wants something *for* us. Our value is not in *what we do*, but in *who we are*."[10]

Boom. Shaka. Laka.

It seems to me that we are chasing acceptance. We are searching for someone to recognize our journeys and understand our paths. If only we knew that God already does! From now on, when you are having someone over (or you are sitting alone in your den floor, buried under a mountain of laundry), I want you to holler, "Cheers to the diaper years!" There is no shame in the momma game, friend. You are not alone. And frankly, you are rocking out at this thing called motherhood.

So today, I encourage you to embrace your own personalized level of crazy. Wear that Tasmanian Devil nametag with pride, girl. Let it all hang out. And remember what my momma always told me: "You don't have to fix your life because it's not about *what* you do. It's all about *who* you belong to."

Now, please excuse me while I go find a dumpster to begin ditching the heaps of mess and attempt to locate the floor in my children's bedrooms. Say a little prayer for me, will you?

Where my fellow Tasmanian Devils at? Love you, soul sisters!

12

Plot Twist: Switchin' Up Our "Have-tos" to "Get-tos"

Before I sat down to begin writing this book, I read approximately seventy-five parenting books, running the gamut of ridiculously insane to Pulitzer-Prize-worthy. I realize that this fact alone qualifies me for the looney farm, but I wanted to be well-versed in the parenting worldview so I was educated before I conversated (more on that later). Well, after exhaustive hours of reading, I can conclusively report to you that there is only one very definitive fact I gleaned that is true for every parenting writer across every platform with every possible line of thinking: Mommin' ain't easy.

This fact is not groundbreaking, no doubt, but sometimes we forget it, push it to the side, or even hide behind it. The truth shall set us free, friends! Some of the hardest things to accept in life (especially in our current world defined by the prettiest, the skinniest, and the most "put together" peeps) is that we might be weak, and—gasp!—we might fail at times, and we might have to actually talk about one (or a thousand) of those tough, chaotic days.

Well, I'll be honest. I'll fall on that sword and wave my crazy flag with pride.

If your wardrobe is incapable of suffering incessant spaghetti and slobber stains, you may want to look elsewhere for your calling in life, or at least begin to release your grip on the latest style catalogs and appreciate the affordable clothing options available at your local Target.

If your idea of a fun Friday night consists of a bubble bath, a bottle of wine, and a binge session of *Real Housewives*, you may want to hang out with some kids around 8:00 p.m. first and receive your very own reality check.

If you are a lady who needs her beauty sleep, well, honey, you just better decide to ditch the quest for the next *Vogue* cover temporarily, because sleep and babies are not typically coinciding trends.

And if you intend to maintain a healthy sex life or even remotely find the thought of sex appealing at 7:52 p.m., once you've finally forcefully strapped and barricaded—that is, sweetly corralled—your children in their beds, you better invest in a reliable babysitter and some kind of magical female sex-drive potion that I would really appreciate you sharing the name of. *Can I get an amen?*

One of my dear friends recently decided to embark on the path to motherhood. She wanted some realistic information about the journey. What does mommyhood *really* mean? Not the pictures you see neatly displayed in brochures or bragged about on social media. The *real* nitty-gritty details. The aspects of the beautiful role that don't naturally meet the eye.

I warned her that we would get to all the mushy, gushy, dream details later, but first I promised to get *real* with her. And today I plan to get real with you as well. This is what I shared. See if you recognize yourself in any of these vignettes. Disclaimer: Don't get bogged down here. This is strictly for solidarity, but as soon as we chest bump on the struggles, we are going to say, "Cheers!" to transforming them into our swan songs of joy—aka that plot twist I teased about in the chapter title.

As mommas …

We have to sling the night masks and beauty rituals in the trash for the foreseeable future. Bottles must be made. Diapers must be changed. Kids cry. They scream—*a lot*. We walk the fine line of insanity and drug-induced euphoria. Mommyhood is unselfishly sacrificing personal comfort for our children's well-being.

We have to develop the most heightened senses imaginable: the ability to hear a tiny sneeze all the way in the basement, as our child sleeps on the second floor of the house with the door closed, while we're watching TV and listening to our husband snore like a freight train. Or the ability to smell a dirty diaper from a park bench as our child plays on a jungle gym approximately thirty feet away. Mommyhood is embarking on an unreal ESP-esque connection with our little ones.

We have to invest in several pairs of ~~glorified pajamas~~ comfy-casual daywear and realize we can dang near conquer the world. Haven't you heard? Yoga pants are the secret location where all of a momma's superpowers truly reside.

We have to embrace *so many* changes. It means having to look at our bodies in completely different ways—children, no matter how we deliver them, will alter our appearance. Stretch marks. Breasts that sag as if belonging to eighty-year-old women. Seemingly permanent bags under our overtired eyes. Those extra ten pounds that we just don't have time to burn off. Trips to the store for Spanx rather than the latest lingerie trend. Mommyhood is all about accepting the changes to our bodies as sources of pride rather than as the battle wounds they appear to us.

We have to postpone personal dreams to nurture our babies at home *or* work outside the home to support a family, while enduring unrelenting, gut-wrenching guilt throughout either path we choose. The guilt game is real. Mommyhood is all about learning to deal with a brand-new batch of self-doubt struggles.

We have to discover the true meaning of work productivity from a toddler. How is it that our little ones can destroy an entire playroom in the few seconds it takes us to flip on a light switch, but some days it takes us two and a half hours to properly unload the dishwasher! #ToddlerProductivityGoals

We have to learn a new language: Boppy, Medela, Tommy Tippee, etc. My head is spinning, and I feel like Rosetta Stone should have prepared us for this! Who even knows what any of these words truly mean? Mommyhood causes us to saunter down totally different aisles in the bookstore to locate "pleasure" reading these days.

We have to be okay with discarding visions of a Martha-Stewart-esque lifestyle unless we flank ourselves with full staffs of chefs, butlers, and nannies. Perfection is for the birds. As long as the kids are happy and healthy, the floors can remain covered in filth, right?

We have to accept that on a daily basis we will hope we don't hear the word *Mommy* again, even though we've spent our entire lives just praying for the opportunity to be called that precious name. The era of the DIY Super Diva has inspired me. Pinterest isn't even ready for my new invention. I plan to install a mommy jar in my home. Each time the little ones say *Mommy* more than once in a five-minute period, they have to put twenty-five cents in the jar. Forget retirement savings, folks. I'm on track to be a millionaire in no time.

We have to survive the crash-course test of domestication. What's for dinner? Are the clothes clean? Where are the keys? Is that a pencil in Junior's *ear*?!

We have to surrender our dining tables to become laundry folding centers, our bedrooms to storage closets, and our pantries to Gerber warehouses.

We have to attempt to wrangle irritable toddlers in the line at the grocery store, praying every second that the scene doesn't result in a Child Protective Services investigation. Homegirl in the checkout line beside us is pulling out her cell phone. Is she phoning in the disruption? Should we alert the elders?

And what the heck do we do when the "terrible twos" turns into "threenager tyranny," which is followed closely by the "formidable fours"? How do we wage our own war on terror—*toddler* terror? Should we spank? What words do we speak to bolster and encourage while attempting to discipline at the same time? Is there even a tried-and-true plan to obliterate nasty behavior? We feel pressured to produce perfect little people who would never dream of misbehaving.

We have to endure intense frustration as we make important life decisions for our children such as school, church, and care. Daycare vs. staying at home. Private school vs. public school vs. homeschool. Pardon me while I curl up in the fetal position in a dark corner. My head is spinning, and I feel sick to my stomach. Will the decisions ever end?! We have to make tough choices that impact friends and family. We have to stand up for what *we* feel is right for *our* children even when others disagree. We have to lie awake at night worrying about whether or not we made the right decision, all while trusting God that His perfect plan will prevail.

We have to wear more hats than a Major League Baseball team. Mommyhood requires us to take on a laundry list (no pun intended) of roles for our little ones: nurse, banker, head chef, boo-boo kisser, party planner, therapist, developmental diva, life organizer, calendar scheduler extraordinaire, and the list goes on and on. Heck, just add on butcher, baker, and candlestick maker for good measure.

....

The greatest things in life result from the toughest challenges.

....

We have to stare at our spouses as if they are roommate-like intruders in our fortresses of silence (aka the master bedroom). It means giving up any hopes of winning the Couple Who Had the Most Sex of the Year award and, instead, vying for the Couple Who Made It to December 31st Yet Again Without Killing One Another honor.

Eventually, mommyhood comes down to releasing our children into the world to spread their wings. A world that increasingly seems to veer farther and farther away from our Lord. It means lying in bed, night after night, weeping as we fear for their safety and well-being. It means finally placing our whole faith in the Lord as we trust in Him alone to guard our children from harm.

Mommyhood is *not* for the faint of heart. It *is* fear-inducing and a responsibility that can make us feel inept and incapable.

But what if we stopped there? What if we continued to reiterate the fact that motherhood is tough at times, but never acknowledged that it is also over-the-moon amazing too? All too often, I think we give motherhood a bum rap. It's easy to sit and sip while lamenting over the loads of laundry, screaming toddlers, and toy tirades, but what if we used that precious time to build one another up and see the light—*God's light*—at the end of our often seemingly endless tunnels?

The greatest things in life result from the toughest challenges. Imagine if Olympic athletes could just bust up in the coliseum the morning of the big race/game/tournament/etc. and knock it out of the park. *No* practice. *No* training. *No* agonizingly long years of failing, succeeding, and perfecting their craft. That would not be nearly as climactic, and news networks would not make any money. Plus, what would we do without all those documentary-style filler videos that keep us pacified until Michael Phelps *does* in fact win for the fourteen-billionth time in a row?

My daddy always told me to dig deep and find my grit, especially when my job title got an upgrade to "Mommy." Grit doesn't show up when the baby is sleeping and the house is clean. Grit shows up in all the times we just discussed. We have to reach out and claim that grit.

Well, I've got grit, how 'bout you?

I have always been told that difficult roads lead to beautiful destinations. There doesn't seem to be a single success story that I've ever read, without a struggle. The same is true with parenting. If we weren't challenged, if we didn't have to constantly tap into our grit, we would become little domestic robots with no purpose but to load up our own little Hot Mess Expresses each morning and do the same song and dance with reality. How boring would life be? How much would we eventually miss those classic chewing-gum-in-the-hair photos or permanent marker covering our freshly painted dining room walls?

I'll tell you, one of the ways I get over this fear is to remind myself that God already knows every single thing that is going to go down in my life and my children's lives. He's not alarmed when things get chaotic because He designed that eons ago. "Your eyes saw my unformed body; all the days ordained for me were written in your book before one of them [even the epic-fail, disaster, 'give me a do-over, GOD!' ones] came to be" (Psalm 139:16).

Life doesn't just end with all those so-called mommy *have-tos*. It's only just begun! There's a whole lot of amazing, life-changing, over-the-moon-wonderful *get-to* moments of mommyhood too. See, I told you we'd get to the "mushy, gushy, light-of-a-thousand-fairies dream" details.

In spite of everything we know to be true about mommyhood, *It. Is. The. Greatest. Role. Of. All. Time.* "Through all the waiting, hoping, planning, worrying, praying, trusting, crying, and celebrating, we become the mothers God wants us to be."[11] Even after all the boogie wipes, diaper rashes, potty accidents, chicken-tender-only diets, spaghetti stains, sticky spills, boo-boos, and sleepless nights, we deep down *love* this journey God has called us to. We wouldn't trade this life for any other in the world, because mommyhood is also all about the greatest parts too.

So what if we changed our have-tos into *get-tos*? "What if we flipped this on its head, and instead of 'have to,' we see that we 'get to'? This simple shift in perspective could change your everything."[12]

We *get* the opportunity to love someone with an unconditional, unfailing, unfathomable, unrivaled love for the rest of our lives.

We *get* the title of Mommy, so when we hear it 1,752 times an hour, that means someone *needs* us.

We *get* chosen as the nurturer, teacher, protector, butcher, baker, and candlestick maker.

We *get* the privilege of prepping the next generation for greatness, even though that means not every day will be a "W" on the scoreboard of life.

We *get* to gaze into the eyes of God's greatest blessings.

We *get* to sacrifice our selfish lives for a greater calling.

We *get* to enjoy all the snuggling, cuddling, and loving we (and our children) can take. Those precious, adorable, little cheeks are *all ours* to kiss to our heart's delight.

We *get* to give the baths, do the laundry, and clean up the messes.

We *get* to savor those life-altering moments of the first step, the first word, and the first time to hear our most prized title proudly exclaim, "Mommy!"

We *get* the *opportunity* to fix the boo-boos, wipe the tears, and hold the hands.

We *get* the slobbery kisses, late-night rocking sessions, and forever best friends.

We *get* to look into the eyes of our little ones and watch as they dream big, laugh hard, and love with the love only *they* can provide.

"'Get to' leads us to gratitude."[13] Mommyhood is a gift from God to remind us that we *are* capable, and that we *get* to love on these precious ones God has loaned us here on this earth. Even when we've surrendered to life's frequent failings, we stop just short of giving up because we know we have—no, *get*—to push forward.

So carry on, mommy warriors. You are incredible. You are blessed. You are brave. You were divinely selected to serve in arguably the most important role imaginable. You *get* to walk upon this incredible, sometimes cray-cray journey. And you can do this through Christ who gives you strength.

CHEERS TO ...

- 🦆 Accepting that chaos is an unpreventable part of motherhood, but realizing that you don't have to let that chaos overcome you.

- 🦆 Commiserating about the fact that parenting, while one of the reasons insane asylums remain open as we speak, is also pretty over-the-moon fabulous. Once you shift your perspective from *have-to* to *get-to*, motherhood really is the greatest role ever.

- 🦆 Learning to cultivate calm and soaking up the moments that matter.

- 🦆 Today's Celebration: Simplify. Look around your home and take the following steps:

  (1) Chunk it—Pretend you're playing Supermarket Sweep. Collect all the items in your home that are no longer necessary, not being used, out of date, or are simply taking up space. Yes, this includes the fermented french fries wedged under the sofa. (Think closets, pantries, cabinets, under the bed, heck, even in the shower—wherever your clutter tends to pile up!) And here comes the fun part: chunk the heck out of all of it and breathe.

  (2) Clean it—It hurt me to type that because cleaning is actually the bane of my existence. However, I've found that if I do something even as simple as Swiffer the floors and wipe down the counters, I feel like maybe I can exist without health services needing to inspect our home's air quality.

  (3) Organize it—Take a look at the remaining items in your home and put them away in a manner that will be easiest for you to find them later. I

am not going to tell you to run to the Container Store and spend your inheritance on clear storage containers and shiny Sharpies. I am going to tell you to maybe *not* store your socks in your planning desk. Or just think about it. Whatever works for you. Friend, if you did any of above steps, give yourself a high-five and a "W" on the scoreboard of #MomLife today.

PART V

Mamarazzis, Pinterest Princesses, and MomBots, Oh My!

Mom Confession: Sometimes I'm so worried about doing it all *perfectly* that I miss out on doing it all *well*.

CHEERS TO ...

TRUTH #5 – You Are Never Going to Be Perfect, but with God's Direction, You Will Be the Best Momma to Your Children

God is perfect, so you don't have to be.

....

Surely there is not a righteous man on
earth who does good and never sins.

ECCLESIASTES 7:20 ESV

....

As for God, his way is blameless; the word of the LORD
is tried; He is a shield to all who take refuge in him.

PSALM 18:30 NASB

13

Pummeling Pinterest Perfection

It's the night before Valentine's Day as I am typing this to you. I'm looking at a list containing the twenty-seven names of my girls' classmates. These four- to five-year-olds are currently nestled in their beds, resting up for the big Valentine's Day shindig at school tomorrow, I imagine.

Meanwhile, I'm staring in trepidation at the hot glue gun as it heats up in the corner, and in this very moment, I have decided to confess something to you: it is *not* getting used tonight, friend. Not on my watch!

My kids may be the black sheep of their classrooms in the morning when Susie Homemaker's little boy shows up with handmade hearts sewn together by what I can only imagine are tiny Valentine fairies she beckons to her home once a year. But I am totally chill about that because I've learned my lesson. I've got my T-shirt. I've collected my $200 on the Mommy Monopoly board of life, and I am wiser for it.

One year, I wasted four hours making homemade Valentines. Pro Tip: Anytime a hot glue gun is involved in the instructions of anything, just walk away. Turn around and walk away. I digress.

This particular Valentine consisted of cups of Jell-O turned upside down with hot-glue-gun-attached googly eyes and pipe cleaners for antennae. The phrase "Happy Valentine's Day, Lovebug!" was taped to the side of each one. Before you throw this book against the wall or pin this idea to your next Valentine's Day Pinterest board, allow me to share with you that my kid could have cared less. Like, she crushed my Pinterest Princess dreams and stomped on my heart as I lay in rejection pose on the dining room floor. My child was three at the time. Here's what I will *not* hear on the morning of her graduation: "My mom is the best. I know this because in 2016, she spent four hours sprawled on the floor of our dining room, looking like an overtired homeless person 'crafting' lovebugs for my Valentine's Day party at school. It was in *that* moment that I knew she loved me."

Are you kidding? My kid is five now. I recently asked her if she liked my lovebug Valentine craft from Pre-K, and do you know what I got? A blank stare in return. *A blank stare, people!* And as a side note, all the other moms shot me death glances for weeks after that little charade because, of course, I bore the label of "*that* mom."

And while we are on this topic, I want to let you in on a little observation I've made. I have never attended a rehearsal dinner where the bride and/or groom stood to acknowledge their mother and uttered any of the following phrases:

"My mom always ties the perfect bow."

"My mom always uses the most appropriate Instagram filters for each occasion."

"My mom always takes the best selfies."

Or my personal favorite: "I really knew my mom loved me because she always cut my peanut butter sandwich into the shape of a heart and tied a piece of burlap twine around the BPA-free plastic silverware in my lunchbox."

I can't, friends. I just can't.

The other day, I kid you not, I stumbled upon a pin entitled "17 Things You Can Do with a Toothbrush Holder." I can't make this stuff up. I want to confess that I immediately had two thoughts: (1) *How about you just use it as a toothbrush holder?!*; and (2) *Really? You could only come up with seventeen? Like, you couldn't whip up another three uses to make it an even twenty?*

Then I realized that whomever designed this pin (God bless you!) spent hours creating this content. They took valuable moments out of their day to share with the world seventeen uses for a toothbrush holder. Meanwhile, I'm over here like, "Who needs a toothbrush holder anyway when you've got a Dixie cup?"

You know what creates more chaos-induced insanity in my life than screaming fits and bath battles? Pinterest. And Instagram. And social media in general. It drives me to the literal edge of a cliff to a point where only Jesus can take that wheel and turn that struggle bus back around.

And you know what else I think? I think Pinterest is actually making us *worse* moms, because behind all those ruffled, mono-grammed DIY aprons donned with just the right amount of burlap and glitter, are moms desperately trying to keep up. Moms who could actually care less if their kids' Valentines are homemade but feel this weird sudden urge to ensure that they are. Moms who wish they could just chill on the couch once the kids are down for the night, but have to meal plan in those perfect little take-out-looking containers for weeks on end. Moms who just need a hug but feel pressured to be insta-perfect at all times.

Pinterest has reignited the cruel game of Keeping Up. "Too often, we unknowingly dream everyone else's dreams. We feel pressured to chase after what's expected, what's comfortable, what appears to be fulfilling to someone else, and what can fit neatly into a box with a bow on top. But you were not made for a box, my friend."[14]

Cheers. To. That.

This is me openly admitting that I've had it with the game of Keeping Up. I actually *do* have a Pinterest page. For a year I didn't pin a single thing. I had all these random followers and not a single pin. You land on my page, and it's all, "Oh hey, girl! I'm gonna teach you how to be the younger version of the Barefoot Contessa!" And then nothing. Not one thing.

I'm not sure what inspiration my precious followers were discovering there before I started pinning, or maybe that was the point! Maybe my totally blank page soothed them in the sea of everything-ness, and they flocked there for Pinterest rehab. You know, to simpler times without all the farmhouse frenzy.

Frankly, my empty page indicated a sleepy momma who didn't feel like sitting up all night on photo editing software, designing the perfectly measured vertical pin to share with you eighteen ways to clean a dirty sink. Nah. I'd rather catch up with *The Bachelor* on ABC.

Are you anything like me? Do you have a love/hate relationship with social media? Does it make you so inspired one minute but also cause you to want to put your head through a wall the next? Well, if so, I have a landmark discovery that I need to share with you today. Did you know that if you log completely out of your social media accounts and turn your phone off, when you turn it back on later, *it's all still there*?!

....

We've got to give up our innate desires for perfection and fall into the arms of God's grace.

....

With this groundbreaking information before us, I have a challenge for all of us: Log out of Pinterest. And Facebook. And Instagram. In fact, log out of all social media for that matter. Just do it. Do it for a day or an hour. If you need a social media step-down program, you do you, girlfriend. I feel like this dynamic is ripe for someone to create a rehab program because social media is without a doubt the world's newest addiction. Investors, where you at?! Let's get that social-media detox app up and running for New Year's!

Okay. Back to our challenge for today. Now close your laptop or turn off your phone. That's it. You are a rock star already. Maybe you need to take a seat for a minute to gather your thoughts. I totally get it. The social-media detox game is real. Now slowly turn around.

Those are your precious children. Reintroduce yourself to them. Hug them. Roll around on the floor and play with them, because you know what's cool about kids? They don't care what the wreath on the front door looks like. They don't have any preferences about the size and/or color of their pumpkin for fall. Or the fifty-seven gazillion hiding spots for that silly little Christmas elf. They aren't concerned with DIY potted plants, and couldn't care less about succulents. Or growing their own herbs. Or shiplap. Or designing their playrooms to look like oceans. I promise. They really couldn't care less about *any* of that.

What they want is YOU. They want *you* to sit with them and read. And maybe even get tickled every now and then. They want *you* to blow bubbles in their faces while they run around outside. They want *you* to snuggle with them for no reason at all. They want *you* to run and pounce in the leaves like it's a giant mountain in their animated play world. They want *you* to launch snowballs at them and watch as they bust on their pant legs for the zillionth time in a row. They want to giggle until their little cheeks turn crimson and it's tough to catch their breath. They want to do what kids do best: *enjoy the little things.*

Maybe we should take a cue from our innocent little ones and return to that carefree joy that we, too, enjoyed so many years ago. We can't let our smartphones outsmart us, friends! We only get so many of those moments, and then it really *will* be just us and our smartphones.

So we've got to give up our innate desires for perfection and fall into the arms of God's grace. Rather than stalking the great minds of the virtual world for crafty inspiration, let's take our kids to the local craft store and stroll aisle by aisle (partly to kill time before naptime, obviously) to become enlightened by the newest crafty notions.

Instead of googling how to make their little lives more perfect, roll around on the floor with them and ask them how *they* want to spend the day. Your kids likely won't remember most of the frou-frou-ish, Pinterest-y moments in life. But they *will* remember all the times you hugged them, kissed them, and chatted about Paw Patrol's latest adventure.

Isn't it convenient for you that those moments are free and *don't* require you pinning anything anywhere?

14

Mamarazzi Mania

Do you remember a time when people actually did things and went places purely for the joy in the experience and *not* to generate Instagram-worthy photos of said experience to post as soon as possible? You know, before we found ourselves tripping over tripods and over-hearing couples arguing about the proper distance to maximize that cool effect in portrait mode? Circa before we all became mamarazzi drones just doin' it for the "'Gram."

Geez, those were the days!

Here's a quick love letter to all my fellow mamarazzis. First, complete solidarity. Just yesterday, I took a photo of the length of my child's hair. I kid you not. I actually asked my child to turn around and face the wall while I snapped a photo of her split ends. I feel certain that twenty years from now, it will be earth shattering that in the photo, it appears her strands grew about 0.000008 of an inch the night before as she slept. I plan to file that photo under "internationally significant; subtitle: life-changing." I can just see it years from now, my daughter and I flipping through old snapshots when all of a sudden said hair photo will pop up, and we will not be able to discuss anything further until after gawking at those precious strands of her hair for at least an hour. I suspect a game of Show and Tell will ensue, followed closely by several choruses of "You've gotta be kiddin' me."

Truth: You are going to feel an uncontrollable urge to capture every gurgle, roll over, and expression that is most definitely gas but has the tiniest shred of possibility at being that infamous first smile. Rather than sweating over collecting montages of moments, be a hoarder of memories instead. Trust me, there's no Canon replacement for that kind of love. When we subconsciously stare at our phones/cameras for long periods of time, we are missing out on all the joy happening just inches behind us. And in case we have forgotten, there are no phones, computers, or tech devices available with a pixel count even close to providing the clearness and quality of the real thing.

....

Rather than sweating over collecting montages of moments, be a hoarder of memories instead.

....

We just talked in the last chapter about tackling social-media-fueled angst, but so many of us strive for a different level of unattainable perfection—the kind where we find ourselves running all over town to create this idyllic life for our babies. You know, the white-picket-fence kind that so many of us dream about as children. Maybe you are in the same boat. You're running yourself ragged trying to be all things to all people. The first mom in pick-up line each day. The wife who sends homemade lunches to work with the hubby. The lady whose front porch planters rival those of an interior-style blogger. The mamarazzi who catalogs every single move and keeps Chatbooks up and running on the regular. I'm exhausted just thinking about it.

The pressure we put on ourselves to keep up is adding to our chaos, and while the thrills of achieving these tiny "Mom-win" perfection moments is addictive, they will not sustain us.

In spite of my mamarazzi ignorance, and as a mom who admittedly has made every effort to create this "picture-perfect" childhood for my kids, I woke up one day and realized that I was throwing all my efforts toward the wrong target board. (And no, I am not referring to my Target Pinterest board—that doesn't even exist, by the way.) Because "parenting is not about God relying on us to be perfect examples for our kids to follow. Parenting is about us relying on God to captivate our child's heart despite all of our mistakes."[15]

So close your eyes and imagine that I am extending my hand to you. Kindly extend yours back, please. We are huddled up on a couch somewhere, chatting about life (like the two best friends I'm envisioning we are, of course). Let's determine how to ditch the psych-ward suits we are destined to don without this little chat.

Friend, we may never be the moms who provide three Food-Network-approved homemade meals a day. We may never be the women who wake at 4:00 a.m. bright-eyed and bushy-tailed, tackling all of our daily chores by 7:00 a.m. We may not win awards for our home organization and cleanliness, although maybe we'll win one for the lack thereof. And you know what? That's all okay. "Imperfection is a gift because it opens a door for us to see His ever-present grace. Right where we are, in every season, His grace abounds."[16]

There comes a point where we must stand vulnerably in the face of God, admit our mamarazzi-mania tendencies, Instagram-influencer inklings, and Pinterest-lack-thereof prowess so that we can fully accept God's grace in the form of these simple yet poignant reminders:

God loves you when you burn dinner.

God loves you when you bring home the groceries and leave the hamburger meat out on the counter for seven hours before realizing it.

God loves you when you lock your keys in the car and cause a scene hollering about it.

God loves you when you wear your shirt inside out all day long and no one cares to tell you.

God loves you when your kid is the only one who doesn't have a handwritten love note from Mommy in their lunchbox at Mother's Day Out.

God loves you when your attempt at a homemade birthday cake is fodder for the profile image on the "Pinterest Fail" Instagram page.

And God even loves you when you forget to take those dang monthly photos of your kid for his first year of life until eight months later, when he walks off the set of the photoshoot.

Because you know what? God loves you all day every single day. And He loves you just the way you are.

15

The Grass Is Greener—
Where You Water It

I went to a movie this weekend, and I'm not even sure I made it to the right theater. Have you ever had this happen? You see a commercial on TV for a new movie and think, *This is going to be amazing!* Then you trek all the way to the theater to watch it, and it's like missing out on the last insane sale computer on Black Friday. Total bummer.

Movie makers, these days, advertise heavily using trailers to attract viewers. They spend about five minutes showing us all the "best" moments from the movie. These genius clips tend to lure us in with this unrealistic expectation that the entire film will be much like the highlight reel—glamorous, exciting, hilarious, *amazing*.

But how many times do we arrive to the theater, settle in with our popcorn, and discover deep disappointment about a third of the way into the film? The trailer contained the only good parts of the movie!

We view highlight reels all the time. Years ago, we only received one "picture-perfect" moment each year in the form of a family's Christmas card. Now we see "Christmas card moments" every single day. If you are a member of Facebook, Instagram, etc., you are a frequent viewer of the highlight reels of life. We see our neighbors', friends', even fellow family members' *best* moments. That perfect meal at a fine dining restaurant. The perfect home. The gorgeous children posed impeccably on a white tufted couch draped with a luxurious fur blanket.

Mom Confession: I am totally guilty of sending out that tufted-couch pic. I know, *guilty as charged,* but what you *don't* know is that literal seconds after that photo was taken, my child threw up all over her pink bouclé dress and our world descended into chaos. We are talking screaming, fit-throwing, good-ole-fashioned Toddler Tyranny.

In fact, hold up. Let's have story time, shall we?

I've alluded to a dark story about my toddler and her crib several times, but I think it bears a little further explanation. Grab yourself a glass of your favorite beverage and curl up with me. I need to let you in on a little mommy moment from a few years back that taught me quite the *load* of a lesson (you'll understand the pun shortly).

It was raining outside and the house was dark. Almost spookily silent. The baby monitor whirred in the background as I attempted to catch a quick cat nap. In the very moment that my heavy eyelids were *just* about to close, I heard the faintest beating sound. It grew louder and louder.

When I sluggishly glanced at the monitor, all I saw at first were dark stripes on the headboard of my daughter's crib. That was just the beginning, because then I noticed her naked booty just shining in the light streaming through her window and her hand slamming against the headboard over, and over, and over.

Up. From. The. Overtired. Mommy. Grave. I. Arose. People!

The second I swung open the door, it hit me like the nauseating stench at the vet's office. *Poop!*

There is really no way to describe the events that followed, other than by saying that I am grateful that God designed insulation to prevent my wild, harrowing screams from alerting the neighbors. I am grateful that my daughter has an interest in the arts—just hoping to refocus little Poop van Gogh on some canvases soon. And I am grateful that my daughter will have no memories of me bawling my eyes out as I scrubbed her entire bedroom with more Lysol and Clorox than is most likely approved by the FDA.

Let me let you in on something else: I did *not* post a picture of this event on Instagram. Didn't post one on Facebook either. Probably could have. *Maybe I should have.* But my point is this: All that glitters is *not* gold. Do not be overwhelmed and discouraged by the pristine photos you see flooding your newsfeeds on satan's gift to the world, social media.

Do not be downtrodden when your attempt at a "fine" meal turns out less than Pinterest-worthy, because my mac and cheese (aka the easiest dish in America) boiled over last night and we survived. (I didn't post a pic of that travesty either.)

Here's even more proof I know what's up with this whole 'Gram-posing game going on. I have dabbled in fashion blogging. I know, I know, everybody's gotta have their vice. Just love me, okay? But I live for the opportunity to dress up, probably because it's a downright holiday when I get to these days. However, if you drop by my house unexpected, you will, without fail, find me in an oversized matching pink pajama set that my dad gave me for Christmas two years ago, which I wash religiously every three days just so I never have to take it off for more than an hour. #TrueStory.

Oh, and one more thing, those gorgeous bloggers who make you hate your body and lust after their insane wardrobes, those same beauties are dragging their poor husbands (or best-friend photogs) out to vacant streets on weekends with trunks full of "outfits," posing for forty-five minutes straight, changing clothes in the backseats of minivans, and deleting 1.5 million outtakes just to get that one photo you see pop up on Instagram bright and early on Monday morning. And then they're driving right back home, climbing back into their trusty old comfy clothes, scrubbing off the makeup, editing said photo for at least another hour, and then settling into their couch for another awesome night of Netflix and chill. Just like everybody else on God's creation. Trust me on this, okay?

I respect that hustle and thoroughly enjoy gaining my newest outfit inspiration from these beautiful ladies, but next time you see that perfect pose and find yourself feeling "less than," promise me you'll remember that I just ripped that smoke screen right off and filled you in on all the real-life, juicy behind-the-scenes deets.

While we're really hammering this point home, why do you think Instagram has filters? Because people wouldn't be nearly as excited to give you a view into their world unless they could filter it to perfection. There's a reason that Facetune and all these other image-altering apps are enjoying international super-craziness right now. Full Disclosure: My favorite filter is Clarendon, and if you choose to follow me on Instagram (hey, girl, hey!), you can bet your bottom dollar that every single one of my pictures have been filtered to death with it. You heard it here first.

So do not feel guilty when you look down and realize that you've been sporting the same pair of nasty sweatpants for the last three days. I think you rock because less laundry = more free time and less water usage, which, if you care, means you just made the water conservation/environmental people all kinds of happy. You go, girl!

Do not get discouraged when you rush up to school for pick-up, discover that you forgot it was picture day, and stare hopelessly at your kid as he trots out wearing a stained T-shirt and ripped cargo shorts. Life happens! If it helps, my mom once let me go to school on picture day with a booger in my nose and a retainer in my mouth. That photo should be outlawed for its hideousness. And, breaking news, I most likely will *not* be unearthing that little gem on social media either.

Remind yourself every time you view these "picture-perfect" moments that you are viewing what this individual deems as one of the "best" moments of their life. If you packed a bag and hung out with them for a few days, I guarantee you might observe spaghetti-stained couch cushions or witness less than "Insta-worthy" moments among family members. At the very least, you would discover that behind closed doors, every human being has bits and pieces of their own movie of life that would disappoint you.

A while back, I took a hiatus from Facebook (aka "Life's Highlight Reel"). I just left it in the dust for a while. I found myself consumed with scrolling endlessly down my home page gawking at beautiful children, gorgeous homes, engagement rings, weddings, fabulous vacations, and the list goes on and on. Often, I would even covet some of the images: *Oh, if only my husband would send me flowers for no reason. … Oh, look at that outfit on that little girl. I've got to get my girls those dresses!* Then God blasted me with this truth: "A heart at peace gives life to the body, but envy rots the bones" (Proverbs 14:30).

Whoa. Game-changer alert.

I have to admit, it *is* fun watching the happy moments in my friends' lives. I want the best for each member of my tribe, but it became too easy to log on each evening and spend an hour or so coveting the blessings of those special people in my life. Meanwhile, I was forgetting to treasure all the beautiful blessings God had provided for *me* and *my* family.

Blessings are like flowers growing in a garden. They are beautiful treasures and gifts to enjoy each day. If nurtured and appreciated, flowers tend to grow and multiply, creating an entire field for enjoyment. But, if neglected and undervalued, they wither and fade away.

....

Never let what you think you may *want* make you forget all the many blessings you *have*.

....

Like flowers, blessings are *not* one-size-fits-all. Just because a friend gets an item you have always wanted, it does not mean that their particular item is part of your "blessing bundle," maybe not for now anyway. In fact, you may be in store for something even greater! God knows exactly what you need. But more importantly, He knows exactly *when* you need it.

The grass is *not* always greener on the other side. And even if it was, it's not the grass God gave you. Spend more time savoring the beauty God has placed in your *own* life and water your *own* grass by acknowledging the wonderful grace that He provides to you daily. If you waste time staring across the fence at your neighbor's yard, you may miss the countless blessings that have been designed just for *you* in your *own* garden.

Don't forget: Never let what you think you may *want* make you forget all the many blessings you *have* right this very second.

So you do you, girl. Post whatever you want, but whenever you're scrolling through all those lovely newsfeeds, remember to be happy for everyone and take everything with a grain of salt.

I've even got some extra hope for you on those *really* bad days. Let's say it is 4:15 a.m., the baby will not go to sleep, and you have had it with life. You are over it and then stumble across your friend's photo of her child displaying the most precious grin you ever did see. Rather than succumbing to satan's temptation of envy, take a minute and consider all the awesome things *you* have to be thankful for:

- God breathed air into your lungs this morning and gave you the precious gift of another day (Genesis 2:7).
- God gives you the freedom to scream out, "Fix it, Jesus!" without judgment all day long. You can call on Him in the parking lot of Ikea just as easily as you can meet Him at the altar on Sunday morning (Ephesians 6:18; 1 Thessalonians 5:16–18).
- God gave you the Bible so that you don't have to hunt on Amazon into the wee hours of the morning, looking for "How to Not Literally Go Insane" books anymore (Psalm 119:105).

- God has given you dreams, girl. And He's gonna provide you everything you need to conquer those bad boys. Today that might mean surviving until bedtime. Tomorrow that might mean leading the PTO or writing a book or starting a business or becoming the first female president. *Who knows?* But I can tell you two things: you were made for greatness, and however God chooses to shine His greatness through you is unique to you and worthy of celebration, friend (Jeremiah 29:11; Philippians 4:13).

- God places people (namely, your kiddos!) in your life who will remind you of just how awesome this life truly is. Those babies will invest in you, which gives you the coolest job of parenting: investing right back in them too (Proverbs 17:17).

- God offers you the kind of love that no man, no baby, no lottery win, no frock off the cover of *Vanity Fair* can give you. And—you got it—not even a brand-spanking-new pair of Spanx faux leather leggings can give you love, girl. God's offering up that "it" kinda love that we've all been searching for since seventh grade. Yes ma'am. That unconditional, unfailing, unadulterated, unfathomable love that no novel could ever hope of capturing (1 John 4:7–8).

- God gives you the kind of grace that makes you wonder why there isn't a book in the Bible titled Zeph-Epic-Fails. He extends you grace even in your darkest hours when you feel like the rest of the world has walked out and slammed that door all up in your face (Romans 5:8; 2 Corinthians 12:9).

- God gave you spiritual gifts/talents to use for His glory that most likely aren't measurable on Instagram. And every single one of God's people said, "Amen." So when you feel like that filter just isn't getting the job done to show off your awesomeness, rest assured that God has prepared you for something so much greater than the world's leading photo app could ever capture anyway (Romans 12:4–8).

- God gave His only Son so that you may be forgiven of your failures and live forever with Him. You have been found. You have been bought for a price. And you have been chosen. Now *that's* the kind of Friend Request Confirmation we *all* need (John 3:16).

- God is currently preparing a home for you that is so incredible—more beautiful and majestic than anything even Chip and Joanna Gaines have ever slung out there (John 14:1–4). (Heaven be a white marble countertop, though, am I right?)

Side Note: None of the items on this list are tangible, material items. You cannot buy any item on this list at Target or pose it on a tufted couch for the 'Gram. You also cannot replace or substitute any item on the list. Meaning, no matter the condition of life you are in, no matter your relationship status, no matter your job title, no matter the amount on your bank statements, no matter how many times your baby screams out into the night—God is *still* faithful to provide your needs each and every day. "[T]hose who seek the Lord lack no good thing" (Psalm 34:10).

CHEERS TO ...

🦆 Living your new favorite phrase: "God is perfect, so I don't have to be."

🦆 Acknowledging that this mythical land of perfection that social media feeds you day in and day out is an outright lie.

🦆 Putting your phone down and releasing yourself of worldly pressures for perfection. Soak it all up and make memories instead of moments for the 'Gram.

🦆 Today's Celebration: Log out of all social media. Plan something fun to do with your kids, solely based off your own inspiration.

Chat with your children about being proud of themselves exactly as they are. And remind yourself that you, too, are amazing just as God created you!

Grab a notebook or journal of any kind, open it up, and list all your blessings on the first page. Your babies. Your home. Your job. Your current manicure color. Whatever you want. List everything that comes to your mind. This is your "Forever Blessings" page that you can look back at any day it seems the rain just won't stop pouring.

Then turn to the next page and date it with today's date. Jot down something (anything) positive that happened today. It can totally be that you woke up today, girl. I get it. Some days are just better left out of the memory books. Keep this daily journaling up for as long as you can. I pray you discover after doing this for a few days or weeks that your life is so worth celebrating! There are amazing moments happening every day that you may be completely overlooking and then forgetting. But when you spend time intentionally reminding yourself of all the ways God has blessed you, you will find that your life is pretty darn amazing just the way it is!

PART VI

Muting All Mommy Shamers

Mom Confession: As if the sleepless nights, busy days, and hormones weren't enough, now I have to deal with mommy shamers and haters too?

CHEERS TO ...

TRUTH # 6 - Your Awesomeness Can't Be Defined by Others

You gotta shake off the haters. Seeking Christ's approval is your only objective. As it turns out, the opinions of Facebook trolls and those awesome "know-it-all" moms are inconsequential—praise Jesus!

....

Am I now trying to win the approval of human beings, or of God? Or am I trying to please people? If I were still trying to please people, I would not be a servant of Christ.

GALATIANS 1:10

16

Mommy Manifesto

M uch like all the high-tech, newfangled, yet somewhat confusing cars we see whizzing around on the roads these days, I think of my mommy plan as a hybrid. I'm not really a working mom since you won't find me in an office from nine to five with my Google calendar dinging me every five minutes. (Although I *do* fancy a leopard stiletto and a project deadline, if I'm being perfectly honest.)

However, I'm not really a gold-star member of the stay-at-home mom group either, since whenever I have a free moment (meaning naptime and when my kids aren't literally bouncing off the walls requiring 24/7 attention), you will find me researching, cranking out legal briefs, and writing love letters, in the form of books, to my newest besties.

But I do know one thing for sure. This little ditty of a discussion, centered around moms and their choice of work, has generated some mighty palpable mommy wars. I happen to think there's a bit of a misunderstanding between the two teams: Team SAHM (Stay-at-Home Mom) vs. Team WM (Working Mom), so it's my mission to clear it up.

It has come to my attention that many individuals truly believe all members of Team SAHM are daily lounging in peace at blissfully blue country club pools while tan lifeguards and teams of apron-clad nannies tend to their ~~bratty~~ delightful progeny. Visions of martinis and bikinis fill people's heads when considering the role of Team SAHM. Um, *wow*. Where is that job application, and are they hiring?! I'm going to leave this right here. I don't think the internet has one clue what a SAHM does, because if they did, they certainly wouldn't associate lounging in a bikini with said occupation.

Cut to the working mom—the savior of her own little world. The lady who just seems to have it all put neatly together. While people stare at these women with righteous condemnation as they make their way from the parking lot to their desks, in perfectly tailored suits/tidy scrubs each day, these fierce ladies are kicking butt and taking names. They surely couldn't have any other care in the world besides world domination, right? Wait. Hold the phone. Have you talked to a WM lately? Because again, stereotypes are for the birds.

These days, it's like we all received PhDs overnight, and instead of just "Mom," we are labeled by one of a million names, typically designed by whatever memes are trending on Facebook that week. There's the "work-at-home mom," the "stay-at-home mom," and the "semi-crunchy-non-vegan-hoola hoop-enthusiast-baby-wearing moms." I can't make this stuff up, people. Have yourself a fun Google session this afternoon if you need a laugh.

There's so much labeling and grouping and "you fit here in this group" stuff going on that we are missing out on embracing each other for all the differences we bring to the table—you know, all the unique qualities that should be helping us and creating bonds between us. I don't fit in to any of the molds that the Twitter mob has designed for moms these days, and I am *so* about that. Turns out, all of us (SAHMs, WMs, hybrid moms, Zumba-or-bust moms, etc.) are motivated by the same number-one goal—to give our babies unconditional love, safety, health, and happiness, however that works best for *our* individual families. The signposts on our journeys are the only things different among us.

So I'm here to make an announcement today. My name is Erin,

and I am a mom. That's it. End of story. If society requires me to have a label regarding my motherhood, well, that's it, friend: *Hi! I'm a mom!* That's my label.

Thank you and good night.

My sudden urge to respond to this whole mom-label crisis got me thinking about things. The Mommy Club consists of some of the most amazing people out there, but here lately, moms everywhere have come under attack—*judgment* seems like a better term. Criticisms about everything from the color of maternity pants to the size of after-baby bumps flood comment sections on blogs. Similar ranting occurs during unwelcomed scolding sessions about proper eating habits and appropriate clothing styles for trend-setting tots. Mommy shamers/haters are popping up everywhere! Side Note: I don't come from a long line of sugarcoaters, so I call them trolls, but you can call them whatever you like.

For example, don't you dare post a photo of your child consuming anything that isn't currently for sale at your local Whole Foods, because the trolls are comin' hard for Cheetos these days, y'all.

In fact, story time! Once at the zoo, I handed out bags of Cheetos to my girls for snack time because #Survival, and I kid you not, I received the most heinous stares from onlookers. I'm guessing these fellow zoo-goers were waiting for me to pull freshly sliced peppers and homemade hummus from my backpack that day. Boy, were they disappointed. I wanted to whip around and exclaim, "For the love of God, people! You are wasting time staring! You'd better call Child Protective Services or PETA or somebody fast to report this travesty of justice!"

As a related side note, I would like to take this opportunity to publicly thank the owners of Pirate's Booty (not sponsored, by the way) for creating a snack that somehow all mommies seem to get on board with even though it's the same dang thing as old-school Cheetos without all the apparently offensive, clothes-staining, fluorescent, *delicious* fairy dust—I mean, orange coating—on top. But who are we kidding? What is childhood without Cheetos stripes down all your favorite pant legs anyway?! What happened to the days when we could saunter down the aisles of the grocery store without being bombarded with five hundred options for each item in the store? Organic. Non-dairy. Non-GMO. No artificial flavors. Lite. Fat-free. Taste-free. My head is spinning.

Retailers should start labeling packages with the following disclaimer: "Will need nutritionist to assist with purchase." Instead of greeters, nutritionists could begin welcoming us at the entrance of the grocery store to accompany us down the aisles. This is the first question I plan to ask the nutritionist assigned to me: "Could you, for the love of Jesus and all things organic, explain to me what the heck GMOs are?" Are they kin to UFOs? Is it a military operative slogan? Are they little cancer pellets hidden away in every bite of my Cheetos? I'm getting worried over here. If you can provide some useful information, could you shoot me a quick message at HelpErinUnderstandGMOs@gmail.com? This is real. Send help. Thanks in advance.

When I run into you at the grocery store, can you guess what I am *not* thinking about? What brand of high chair does she use? Does she co-sleep? Did she have a quinoa and kale salad for lunch, chased down by a green smoothie? To be honest with you, I could care less about any one of those things. Rather than accosting the produce stocker about the origination and growth habits of Hass avocados, you will find me filling my cart with items that do not require such intense interrogative research. You know, items we've all been existing on since the beginning of time.

My momma, bless her sweet soul, fed me Kellogg's Corn Flakes, M&M's, and even let me sneak sips of orange soda from time to time. And here's your breaking news alert for today: I survived that glorious childhood. Gasp! Pre-high-fructose-corn-syrup hysteria, our world was such a wonderful place. We reveled in our blissful ignorance, and we survived. We made it. The corn-syrup centaurs didn't come devour us in our sleep, people!

I'm all about teaching our children healthy, clean eating, but can we do so without engaging in discussions that result in righteous condemnation? If anyone wants to write a book summarizing all of these "uber-healthy" options and exposing all the superfoods in a graph-like format for ease of reference, that'd be great. (Quick request—provide a dictionary in the back, and write it on a level that even my kindergartner can understand.) I'll be your first buyer.

Rather than agonizing over the origination of the *foods* that enter our children's bodies, let's spend more time focusing on the *words* they hear, the *things* they see, and the *places* they go. If we spend more time focusing on *that* version of input in our child's lives, we will be doing our world a much greater service.

I could write an entire treatise addressing all the topics that generate mommy shaming these days, but I'll stop here for now. The purpose of this was to lead us toward a constructive discussion about doing away with mommy shaming once and for all! It's always easier to tear down than to build up. Just ask your precious toddler—and I'm not talkin' about Legos here, mommas. This tyranny of torture has to stop, friends! It's time to say "Bye, Felicia!" to all this nonsense.

Parenting is kind of like shooting from the hip. Children keep us super busy, on our toes, *and* on our knees in prayer at all times. Blindly swinging and praying that we hit a home run daily. If there was a "perfect mom game plan," trust me, we'd all have a copy and we'd all be in receipt of annual awards. I have realized this whole shaming problem originates from us not understanding one another's journeys. Or maybe it's better described as the *disinterest* in understanding one another's journeys.

The second we become moms, we've hit the jackpot, won the award and achieved the highest honor! We sort of neglect to realize that others may have walked different paths. Maybe they struggled. Maybe *they* suffered. Like snowflakes, no two pregnancies and no two mommy stories are identical. Each path has thunderstorms *and* sunrises along the way. The truth is, there is no perfect story. No tale worthy of identic replication. *No perfect mommas!*

What if we took a minute and really looked at the truth about motherhood? What if we considered all the glorious highs but also took a look at the valley of lows? If we took more time considering the feelings of others, all the while acknowledging that their path may be very different from our own, we would become much more understanding of one another. Kindness will reign once again.

The moral of this manifesto is this: Mommyhood comes in all shapes, forms, and sizes. No two mommas have the exact same story. We've all fought the good fight in some way or another. We all have unique preferences, tastes, and theories about life. We've got to be sensitive to each other's journeys and appreciate one another for our differences. "If our true value is based on how God sees us, then it is easier for us to be honest with others, because what they think about us or how they respond no longer defines us."[17]

So I want you to know something today, momma. You are awesome. You brought a baby into this world through birth or by entering the beautiful ministry of adoption. Your story is unique and laudable. You don't have to worry about anyone else's journey or what they think of yours, because yours is perfect just the way God wrote it.

17

Brouhaha to Kumbaya

Did you know that hosting and/or participating in a baby shower is now considered a felony in twenty-seven states?

Of course, I'm kidding. But if you find yourself killing time during your nap today (Ha! We can dream, right?) and run across a seemingly innocent video of a gender reveal party, please, for the love of God and all things pink and blue, do not, I repeat do not, read the comments underneath said video. There are not enough mad-face emojis in the whole world to adequately combat the ignorance that resides there.

These days, a simple Facebook status will send some people to the brink. In layman's terms, these people are losing their ever-loving minds on a Tuesday afternoon, at two o'clock, when they could be doing anything else in the world, yet they feel the need to sit and write a treatise on proper balloon etiquette—as if anyone cares. Friends, mommyhood is tough enough on its own. We don't need enemies in our own camp. We need to strive to empathize, encourage, and empower one another to greatness! We've got to have a little more Kumbaya mommyhood and a lot less Brouhaha mommyhood!

It seems like each one of us is always fluctuating between two very divergent parenting emotions on any given day: (1) the "I know everything, so everybody else take several seats and chill" mode; or

(2) the "I know nothing and I plan to go hide in a cave for eighteen years … wake me up for graduation" mode.

There will be times when we feel like God has chosen us to be the spokesperson for all mommas. In those scarce moments, it will feel like we have it all together—we got to school on time, the lunches were perfectly packed, the outfits were clean and ironed, and no one had a meltdown in carpool. Those are the days, man. The days when we get mad that any other human could possibly think they know more about being a mom than we do because we are the best. Ain't no one greater.

But there will also be a ton of moments when we look in the mirror and see the craziest, most-harried shell of a human staring back. There are definitely going to be times that we feel like hiding in the basement is our safest option. Here's the thing: There's really no way to tell what kind of a mode another momma is in—today she may be the leading expert on breastfeeding; tomorrow she may be sobbing on the floor of her therapist's office. And this is exactly why we have to be kind *always*.

Paul teaches us in Romans 12:16 to "live in harmony with one another." If we spend all our time judging and criticizing one another, that doesn't leave much time left for harmonizing.

And what about the Golden Rule? Sometimes I feel like we, as mommas, reserve mention of the Golden Rule for toddler story time before bed. We forget that the age-old adage applies to *all* of us. Let's remind ourselves what it says (out of the context of The Berenstain Bears and more in the context of running into Jane in the grocery-store line).

"So in everything, do to others what you would have them do to you" (Matthew 7:12). Did we really catch that word *everything*? Jesus said we are to do unto others as we would have them do to us in everything we do. Which means our Facebook comments are included; the things we say about our fellow mommas are included; and yeah, even the comments we make in front of our children are included in *everything* too. "For the mouth speaks what the heart is full of" (Matthew 12:34).

Then it hit me. How do my children see me treat other moms? What do my friends say about me when I'm not around? How are they beginning to define my reputation and legacy? If we focus our hearts on Christ, His grace is bound to flow out, because we've got that light and we've gotta let it shine, girlfriend! When we care more about loving others, we don't have time for gossip sessions, judgy-wudgy vibes, and silly games. And what's more, we won't want anything to do with all of that.

The next time you feel tempted to comment on another momma's parenting choices, take a quick second to imagine how you would feel if you knew someone was gossiping in kind about you. How would you feel to know that someone was lashing out at you instead of picking you up?

Here's a quick suggestion for combatting those feelings. Did anybody else's momma browbeat them with the old adage "Think before you speak. If you don't have something nice to say, don't say anything at all"? Side Note: I love you, Mom! My sweet momma never missed an opportunity to whisper those words in my ears. I can't tell you how many times I have literally drawn blood inside my mouth after biting my inner lip during a conversation. You know that feeling when you just want to scream whatever is on your mind in that moment?

We are all guilty of speaking without thinking from time to time. It's human nature. But the Bible tells us to spend our time on other things: "Finally, brothers and sisters, whatever is true, whatever is noble, whatever is right, whatever is pure, whatever is lovely, whatever is admirable—if anything is excellent or praiseworthy—think about such things" (Philippians 4:8).

Well, there you have it. There's Paul with another mic-drop moment of his very own, friends. From now on, no matter if we are using our mouths or our keyboards to communicate, let's all commit to take a minute to remember this internet-famous T.H.I.N.K. acronym (kudos to whomever created this) before we speak following these guidelines:

T – Is it True?
H – Is it Helpful?
I – Is it Inspiring?
N – Is it Necessary?
K – Is it Kind?

If you answered yes to these questions, then share that message with the world, friend! If you answered no to any question, it might be best to take my momma's sage advice and say nothing at all.

When you begin to act with these thoughts in mind, your kindness will spread. When tempted to react, take a moment and collect your thoughts. You can inspire kindness, one person at a time. If you take a kind approach with those who are unkind, eventually you will wear them down or they will get bored with not receiving a reaction and move on. Take back the power by resisting the urge to give these haters any kind of reaction!

What we all really want is to be understood. We desire for everyone to walk a mile in our shoes, checking out everything we've got going on. It seems that if we truly want to be understood, we must extend that grace to others as well. We all love our babies with everything inside us. We would give our right arms if it meant our babies benefitted. We all want what is best for our children. Our primary goal is the same—even if that vision is not identical to others. We all want to be loved. To be seen. To be understood. To be given grace. We are all working our butts off to survive. Some days are good. Some days are worthy of mention in the #EpicFail encyclopedia. We aren't perfect. Not a single one of us. But we are the very best choice for our little ones.

We are all tasked with loving the heck out of these incredibly adorable, albeit sometimes craze-inducing, blessings God has bestowed upon each of us. Why can't we unify in the fact that we are all mommas at the end of the day? Let's love each other in spite of our differences. Let's learn from one another and grow from new experiences. Let's encourage one another rather than tear each other down all the time. Let's be the change that each of us so desperately wants to see. Encourage other moms. Pray for them. Love them.

You have been given treasures in the form of your precious children. Thank God each day for your incredible blessings and commit to living a life of love in front of them. Provide them a legacy worth replicating. And when the goin' gets tough, remind yourself to take a second and do these three things:

1. Educate before you conversate.
2. Empathize before you criticize.
3. Edify before you terrify.

Breathe this prayer each morning, before you rise, to guard your heart and your lips for the day: "Set a guard, O Lord, over my mouth; keep watch over the door of my lips" (Psalm 141:3). Judging will get us nowhere. We've gotta oust the hate and love each other through it all. Mommas unite! "She speaks with wisdom, and faithful instruction is on her tongue. She watches over the affairs of her household and does not eat the bread of idleness. Her children arise and call her blessed" (Proverbs 31:26–28).

Now that we know exactly how to tame our tongues and stand firm in who we are, let's hunker down on how to deal with those haters, girl. Let's look at what the Bible says about encouraging those folks to take several seats.

18

Haters Gonna Hate

This weekend I witnessed some mind-blowing, ludicrous "momma drama." You know what I mean. One momma posted an Instagram photo, followed by another momma slamming her for the improper use of safety pins on the back of her child's dress. Wait. What?! Is there a world-renowned safety pin expert I wasn't aware of? Does she have a published book on this topic? As an avid reader, I feel inspired to add it to my collection. Or if not a book, is there at least a webinar? If so, present yourself, you safety pin genius, you!

Like me, some of you amazing moms may have experienced a form of "shame" or unnecessary unrest throughout your parenting journey. Maybe you have even experienced the direct criticism of a "hater." By the way, I'm unsure who should be credited with coining the phrase "haters gonna hate." Maybe Taylor Swift deserves the honor because of the lyrics in her hit song "Shake It Off." Either way, the phrase has gone viral and is quite provocative. I hear people use it all the time in the grocery store, at school, even at church!

In life, there will be people who misunderstand us or do not grasp the meaning of our journeys. This could pop up in unrequited friendships with other women, passive-aggressive remarks on mommy blogs, or even a comment about balloon safety. Unfortunately, these are not new problems. Jealousy, self-esteem issues, and anger are tough-stuff issues that people have dealt with for ages.

These bullies we encounter on a daily basis are plagued by one or several of these emotions.

So I beg of anyone willing to listen, please wake me up when the troll tribe finally does us all a favor and kindly exits stage left, will you? These days, I find myself thinking more often than not, *Can't we all just get along?*

Everyone has critics in life, but these haters have taken it to a whole new level. They voluntarily and intentionally try to hurt others through their words or actions. For some reason, these individuals have become desensitized to the feelings of others.

I've also noticed a new but very related problem. It isn't just mouths that lower the boom these days; it's keyboards too. "The internet has provided our generation with newer and greater opportunities to invite unnecessary conflict and drama into our homes."[18] It has become way too easy to hide behind a computer screen while wreaking havoc on even the least suspecting victims. Some days, Facebook, Twitter, and other social media sites are just a tad hostile, to say the least. Our parents never had to worry about this new-age righteous condemnation. They were safe until they ran into Judgy Jane at the grocery store.

The typical demographic for these hater/shamers is either overtired, angry-at-the-world mommas or individuals who have never even birthed a child! I envision overworked and underappreciated souls lurking in dark corners of their homes as they type venomous hurtful messages to unassuming recipients on social media. Rather than the dreaded hand, foot, and mouth quandary, these folks are enduring a scary bout of Foot *in* Mouth Disease!

And there are countless triggers for haters. These people tend to lack self-esteem. They find the successes of others intimidating. They could be carrying unrelated emotional baggage, or there may simply be a miscommunication between the two of you that needs sorting out.

Whatever the excuse, it is never acceptable to cause pain to another. I promise it will help you to remember that the hate you experience is not about you. It is all about the hater and the issues they are experiencing in their own lives. When people judge you, it does not define who you are; it defines who they are.

I have to take this opportunity to throw down a little truth grenade again, because no time like the present. Why the heck do we care what others think anyway? Like, really, why? Why do we even give them one second of our very precious time? I am here to tell you that you do not have time for those shenanigans, sister. You have got much bigger fish to fry than caring about what Frieda on Facebook thinks of your child's multicolored fingernails. So take a hot second and twirl on those haters, girl. Always think of this verse again whenever a hater engages you: "Am I now trying to win the approval of human beings, or of God? Or am I trying to please people? If I were still trying to please people, I would not be a servant of Christ" (Galatians 1:10).

Mic drop.

Thank you and good night.

You don't have to respond to these individuals. The second you lose your temper or engage in unkind words, you lose your witness and that's too much of a risk to take, momma. The next time someone comes trolling, I want you to envision me looking you in the eye, maybe gently shaking your shoulders, and saying, "Who cares? Who made them queen/king of the world?" Answer: Nobody. No, not one.

Be gone, Facebook Frieda. With all your fingernail-hatin' games, because Paul, in his infinite wisdom, just gave us the exact tool we need to twirl on haters like you. We are *not* trying to win your approval. So take several seats, lady.

....

When people judge you, it does not define who you are; it defines who they are.

....

These haters, like hypothetical Frieda, are looking for a reaction. They want us to engage them on their level. Rather than paying these individuals back with hasty, mean words of our own, let's love them to Christ. Let's forgive them, often, even without an apology, as Christ did on the cross when He said, "Father, forgive them for they know not what they do."

Even though it can seem unbearable to deal with the criticism, negativity, or hurt that others bring into your life, you can make efforts to change the cycle. You are only responsible for your own actions and reactions. You can pray for God to intervene, and, in the meantime, lean on Him for strength.

So whenever you encounter your next momma hater, know-it-all mom (we all know one or two), or the overbearing (yet often well-meaning) physician, remember that their words and/or actions are of no consequence in the bigger picture of life. God is the ultimate judge and jury. It is His favor, and His alone, that you seek. God did not design you, or them, for perfection. He designed you, and them, for a purpose. And your purpose, as it relates to your parenting, is to love your child the way God loves you.

People will attack you. *Pray for them anyway.*

People will try to hurt you. *Extend grace anyway.*

People will attempt to rob you of your joy. *Love them anyway.*

You know the feeling when someone smiles at you? It's next to impossible not to smile back. The next time you encounter a hater, remember this quote: "Haters gonna hate, but I will just keep on lovin' them to Christ!" "For if you forgive other people when they sin against you, your heavenly Father will also forgive you. But if you do not forgive others their sins, your Father will not forgive your sins" (Matthew 6:14–15).

CHEERS TO ...

- 🦆 Being the change you wish to see in the world. Kicking the haters to the curb. It can be tough business, but God asks you to take the high road in all those situations. So what is the opposite of being a hater? Being an encourager. Paul shares in 1 Thessalonians 5:11–23 some aspects of encouragers that you can strive to possess daily, a "Checklist for Encouragers," if you will.[19]

1. Build Each Other Up – Just like we teach our toddlers, if you are nice, someone will be nice to you. This logic should be the standard on *and off* the playground (v. 11).
2. Respect Others – Aretha Franklin sings a little ditty about this. Give it a listen in your five-minute margin moment today for a boost of R-E-S-P-E-C-T realness (v. 12).
3. Live in Peace – I think ladies who "let bygones be bygones" should be the new definition of "cool moms." I'll leave it out there for a group vote, but those peeps are the real MVPs, if you ask me (v. 13).
4. Uplift Those Who Are Struggling – Rather than overstating the universal truth "the struggle is so real," listen up next time that mom is venting. She just may be secretly begging you to show her a little extra mom love today (v. 14).
5. Be Patient – This is a particularly tough one for many. Mom Confession: This is really tough for me. Encouragers especially want to look at planning ahead for extra crazy times. This way you are prepared to handle worrisome situations with grace (v. 14).
6. Resist Revenge – Haters are the worst. And most of us don't do well with all that drama. But how can we expect God to "do well" with us, if we can't forgive their failures too (v. 15)?

7. Be Joyful – Think of Buddy the Elf. Just do it. Close your eyes and get Will Ferrell in his little green outfit dancing in your head. Now think about how awesome God truly is. If you aren't smiling by now, I don't even know what to tell you because smiling is my favorite (v. 16).

8. Pray Continually – All day. Every day (v. 17).

9. Give Thanks – Saying thank you is the best way to remind yourself of all the reasons you have to be thankful in the first place (v. 18).

10. Count On God for Help – You don't have to live by your own strength but through God's power. It's okay to let out a "Woo-hoo!" right about now (v. 23–24).

PART VII

From Worrier to Warrior

Mom Confession: I'm scared. And nervous. And a hot mess 99.87 percent of the time. The mommy-manic-mode struggle is so real, y'all.

CHEERS TO ...

TRUTH #7 - You Can Give Up Googling and Look to the Word

Turning to God is a way better plan (and much less expensive) than therapy, anxiety meds, and sixteen glasses of Pinot ever could be.

....

"For I am the LORD your God who takes hold of your right hand and says to you, Do not fear; I will help you."

ISAIAH 41:13

19

Worrywart to Christ Cohort

One of the coolest things about motherhood is the fourteen billion new things we get to worry about. Am I right?

Did you know that if you Google "foods you should not eat while pregnant," every single food option known to man will pop up in a nauseatingly long litany of hits? Just so you know, there is some author in some room, somewhere in the world, who will happily tell you that Frosted Flakes are strongly discouraged during pregnancy. I need you to know that I personally disproved this theory though, friends, because my baby and I survived off that delicacy for at least three months of my first pregnancy.

When it comes to all things parenting, especially motherhood, the Google Blair-Witch-esque factor is sky high. Google's tagline should honestly read "Google: Providing mothers one million reasons to be scared out of their minds and keep their physicians on speed dial at all times."

Allow me to take this moment to offer a subtle suggestion: Please kindly ask your husband, best friend, and/or cable provider to disable Google for you right this second, or at least install some form of mommy-deets block, because no matter what you put in that little query box, it's going to come back with one of two answers: "you will die immediately" or "you will require a lifetime of therapy."

When I was first delving off into motherhood, I literally Googled everything. I'm guessing you did too. I Googled what position I should sleep in, what to do if I didn't feel my baby kick in the last twenty minutes, and even how to get my kid to hug me back.

I spent an entire afternoon just on food queries, which, looking back now, makes me feel like I need to guest star on some sad talk show to vent about my insanity. Because I was going to be the GOAT ("greatest of all time") of the Mommy Club, I jotted down a list, on a paper towel, of every food-related item I could *not* have and tucked that bad boy in my purse for immediate reconnaissance. I became "that" friend, and everyone began emailing me menus days and weeks prior to meal outings to ensure that your girl had made up her mind on a selection prior to sitting down; this was obviously to prevent the forty-five-minute sessions it had been taking me to order prior to the homework plan. Side Note: We have to give up feta? Who came up with that? That's just motherhood abuse.

If I stopped there, you might still think I was somewhat normal with my googling, and I am not about deceiving you, girl. So I will let you in on a few more of my most embarrassing Google searches of all time: "What happens if the power goes out during labor? Can they still see the baby? If not, what do they do to find it?" This search was accompanied by another fave: "What happens if my doctor has a wreck on the way to the hospital, and I am forced to deliver my baby with the assistance of an individual who has not passed my 178-page questionnaire regarding doctor/patient suitability?"

Guys, all of these searches occurred before I even showed up to the hospital. Bye, forever.

I will spare you my remaining doomsday daydreams, but I have to hope that maybe you've wondered similar things from time to time. Or maybe you can help me feel better by saying you did? Truth Bomb: There's not one thing I can do if the power goes off at the hospital. And I cannot prevent my doctor from wrecking on the way to the delivery room, although you should know I pray for you daily, Dr. Robinett.

God is the author of my story. All those afternoons I sat drinking babycenter.com-approved beverages and lounging, not so comfortably, dreaming up all these off-the-wall doomsday scenarios, were a righteous waste of my time. I quickly discovered that I'd really be robbing the greatest playwright of all time the recognition He deserves if I continued masquerading under this assumption that if I just Google it enough or research it enough, I'll get it all figured out.

So here's the good part. Did you know that if you consult the Bible for whether to eat Frosted Flakes or sushi or listeria-laced sandwich meat, and/or what happens if the power goes out during labor, you will find the same answer every single time?

Trust God.

That's it. Just do it. Consult God, not Google, my friends.

There is a reason that God doesn't have a separate encyclopedia laying out every single answer to every one of our questions, because the Bible addresses what to do in *all* of our late-night worry-induced Google sessions: "Trust in the Lord with all your heart, and lean not on your own [or Google's] understanding; in all your ways acknowledge Him, and He will direct your paths" (Proverbs 3:5–6 MEV).

....

Consult God, not Google.

....

I don't know about you, but I'd much rather be known as a Christ cohort than a worrywart any day of the week! Obviously, we have to be smart about our choices in pregnancy and motherhood, but if we think we will be any kind of help to our babies if we are booking hours on end with the authors in the Google world—again, we gotta check ourselves before we wreck ourselves.

I love how my grandmother approaches this whole thing. Throughout my life, whenever I have had fears or worries, I have headed over to Mamaw's house. She is truly my divinely inspired calmer. She speaks with such confidence, yet her tone is comforting. Mamaw is my life's perma-hug.

One day, I drove to her house in a mad fury, desperately needing my worry-wizard's latest revelation. We sat on her porch, as we tend to do, in her comfy Cracker-Barrel-approved rocking chairs. We rocked, and I bore my soul, lamenting over every last detail of my current troubles.

She paused to get us some refreshing sweet tea—because #SouthernLife—and after a few swigs, she slapped her hand on the arm of her chair. She gazed up at me with her sweet eyes locked in on mine and said, "Baby, worrying is like these old rocking chairs. It'll give you something to do, but it's not gonna get you anywhere."

So there's that, ladies. Take it straight from the mouth of my worry-wizard herself. Worrying isn't gonna get us anywhere.

Mommyhood is overwhelming. A whole lotta whelm. Like, all the whelm. And we worry. We worry about whether we are using the right pacifier. We worry if the kid in preschool sitting next to our kid is saying mean things. We worry about college choices. I could go on and on.

Worries are nothing but thieves in the night. They taunt us. Tempt us and keep us from slumber. For what? What if we stopped believing that we have to have it all figured out? What would happen if we finally dropped this veil of unwarranted security and, again, let our crazy hang out a bit?

We don't have any ounce of control over whether or not our children are going to "be okay," or whether they are going to graduate, get married, have kids, and live happily ever after. It's not possible for us to determine the future, *but God can.* God can do anything. "Jesus looked at them and said, 'With man this is impossible, but not with God; all things are possible with God'" (Mark 10:27).

So often we forget that it doesn't even matter if we have it all together. We can spend all our mornings fretting over the details, or we can give it to God. We can waste all our nights staying up worried about tomorrow, or we can embrace the grace God has given us today. From now on, look upward, not inward, for your security on this earth.

When your child spikes a 103-degree fever at 4:00 a.m., there's nothing you can do but shove in some Motrin, call the doctor's after-hours line, and holler, "All things are possible with God!"

When the checkbook won't balance because kids + adults = expensive, you need to state, confidently, "All things are possible with God!"

When your toddler tinkles on the floor like an untrained puppy, crushing your dreams of finally checking the painstaking potty-training process off your to-do list, and all you want to do is bang your head against a wall, you should scream, "All things are possible with God!"

I will tell you exactly what I do when I worry about something, in hopes that this will help you too. Take these three easy steps:

1. Stop, drop, and pray;
2. Share your fear with someone, preferably a trusted friend in your tribe or loving family member; and
3. Ask that person to pray with you and for you.

"So, don't worry about tomorrow, for tomorrow will bring its own worries. Today's trouble is enough for today" (Matthew 6:34 NLT).

Turn your worries over to the Lord. He'll be up all night anyway.

20

Bedsprings Baptist

I t's all fine and good to be prepped on the fact that God's in control. Stop googling! And pray, girl. Pray! But what do we do when those fears turn into our reality?

As I am typing these words, our country is experiencing the worst outbreak of flu in my lifetime, and due to this mommy-nightmare-inducing fact, my family has not left the house—meaning not even attended church—in three weeks. Cue all the shock and gasps. *I get it.* But we are killing the game at Bedsprings Baptist, folks!

Which leads me to my next confession. I started out as a helicopter mom. Wait. I still am one. Strike all of that. I am a recovering/still-kinda-sorta helicopter mom. Allow me to explain.

This will shock most of you, but my three-year-old (the younger of my two girls) had never been to the grocery store until rather recently. I know. Pick your jaw up off the floor. It's insane. I get it. *Can we still be friends?* If you knew her, you would know exactly why. The world is her stage. She's never met a stranger, but the sweet little thing is a tiny bull in a big ole china shop wherever we go.

Well, she went for the first time a few months ago—and things did *not* go well. Let me just say, I really began to think that maybe I had been *correct* in keeping her tucked away at home, shielded from all the dangers of the world in that moment. Okay. Here's what happened.

We only had five minutes to grab three items. You know the drill, whip 'em out of those car seats and dart in and out of the grocery store faster than the Flash. Except for when that doesn't work out.

Once inside, I grabbed a buggy. Kids say, "No buggy, Mommy!" They want to walk like big girls (imagine an eyeroll emoji here). This would end up being our demise, people! So my little ones start meandering behind me. As we head down an empty aisle, my youngest decides to bolt for it. Just imagine that classic *Baywatch* scene (sans teeny-weenie swimsuit) where the person is totally delusional and running in slow motion with no care in the world.

She got up to top speed, turned her head to look at something on the shelves, and *nailed* that silly buggy we had, right on a broken rusty piece under the handle. Blood started gushing *everywhere*. We are talking crime-scene blood. I mean, in the future paramedics should be required to study this case. ALL THE MOPS ON AISLE SEVEN, PEOPLE!

Ironically, we were in the paper-towel aisle, and I couldn't even grab one because I had to get this kid out of there and to the hospital. No time to pay for silly paper towels when your kid's got a gusher! So instead of doing the *smart* thing and dabbing her with a paper towel to assess the bleeding (before bolting like a college girl after a bad date), I buried her little head in my chest and sprinted for the door. It's a blue wonder how my other toddler managed to make it to the vehicle unharmed after I sped off like I had just robbed the joint. *The horrors!* I am realizing as I type this that I most definitely still have a classic case of PTSD related to this incident, y'all. All you therapists hit me up, mmmkay?

But don't alert the elders just yet, because this story *does* have an okay ending. After the three-minute drive to our house, a soak in the tub, an entire bottle of hydrogen peroxide, a Band-Aid or two, and gobs of TLC, my baby returned to normal. She survived. To my knowledge, everybody in a three-mile radius of Publix survived. Thank God for tiny miracles.

This crazy story led me to several epiphanies, but I'm only sharing one today: Obsessing over all the little things that *could* go wrong with our babies and overexerting our control is *not* the best way. We are not allowing God to use instances like the brutal paper-towel-aisle incident to help us in our parenting. As Todd Wagner says, "Worrying is believing God won't get it right."

Helicopter-mom life is much like being a backseat driver. Those folks mean well, *I'm sure*, but doesn't it really just annoy the driver? Like, to the point that they just want to slam their foot on the gas pedal and drive off an embankment somewhere? Well, I think that's what my little one might have been trying to subconsciously tell me that day. And she's exactly right. I have to fight the urge daily to be a backseat driver to my Savior! All those years of stowing my little one away like Rapunzel were silly. All those incessant talks about how to walk in a grocery store, where to walk, when to walk, and what to do while walking were all in vain until I let her experience it on her own.

As mommas, it is so tempting to wrap our babies in bubble wrap and play with them like fragile little dolls. We spend hours coaxing our little ones to sleep, and then what do we do? The second they dose off into restful slumber, we get up in their faces, shine our cell phone flashlight up in their nostrils to make sure their nose hairs are moving back and forth indicating proper breathing. But like that backseat driver, we are really just exerting that extra ounce of control that we are so desperately clinging to. Ouch. I said it. That's me to a tee.

This "let go and let God" thing is coming *really* slowly for me when it comes to my kids. Anyone else? I'm *not* suggesting that we throw our kids in the street and wait to see what happens, but I *am* suggesting that after we've given them instruction, let's do our best to stand back and let them be. They are going to make mistakes. They may even run into buggies at one hundred miles per hour, nail their forehead, and gush emergency-room-status blood everywhere, but that's all a part of learning. For them and for us too.

We have to trust Christ to see us through everything we encounter, reminding ourselves in every moment that He has already gone before us! He knows what is lurking behind that corner up ahead, and He has prepared the means for us to overcome it in His name. So while we've really been enjoying our time at Bedsprings Baptist, I'm reminding myself today that God will take care of us *outside* the house too.

SIP ON A CUP OF HE'S GOT THIS

"May the God of hope fill you with all joy and peace as you trust in him, so that you may overflow with hope by the power of the Holy Spirit" (Romans 15:13).

If you thought my ditty about the Publix fiasco was less than legendary, allow me to share with you when God *really* showed this momma what's up with worrying.

About six months ago, Annalise came down with two or three ear infections in a row (unrelated to her epic-fail Publix buggy moment). While very common for children, this was a little extra concerning because of the extreme amounts of antibiotics we were forced to pump into her little body to cause these infections to subside.

One night, we returned home from an outing and Annalise began screaming in pain. We all assumed her ear was flaring up once again, until we noticed her lying on the ground shaking. I took her in my arms, and we laid on the floor for what felt like hours. She wasn't settling, friends. It was way past bedtime, so I suggested maybe sleeping would give her some comfort. When we stood to go to her room, she collapsed. I thought she was pulling the threenager-ain't-gonna-do-it-game, but this was serious. My baby could not move her legs. I would love to report to you that it was a fluke and she stood unassisted moments later—but she didn't. *For days.*

I have never experienced something so scary. The prospect of my healthy little one suddenly and inexplicably losing the ability to walk was more than my little momma heart could bear. I spent days dreaming about what our new life would look like with the prospect of her not walking again. But after a litany of doctor's appointments, testing, etc., we discovered that rather than a life-altering illness, she had experienced a rare allergic reaction to the medication she was taking for her ear infection, rendering her incapable of using her legs at times. Y'all, who the heck knew that was even a thing?

Can we be real for a moment? There are so many crazy things that happen all the time with our little ones that we are going to have *no* control over. They are going to run crazy high fevers. They are going to fall off things, and jump off things, and run into things. All. The. Things. If we could spare them every little ounce of pain, we would, but God's got that end of the deal.

One night, when I was channel surfing (around the time of this allergic reaction ordeal), I ran across a McDonald's commercial that had nothing to do with my predicament, but I loved the tagline: "Sip on a Cup of I've Got This."

Whoa. That really stopped me in my tracks. I *live* for catchy slogans, people. Then it made me think about other trendy sayings such as "God doesn't give us anything we can't handle." *Well, of course* God gives us things we can't handle on our own—like infertility, and sickness, and colicky babies at 4:00 a.m., and seemingly healthy toddlers who can't walk for a few days to remind us that in those moments, when *we* can't handle it, *He* can. This is yet another reminder that He is our enough-ness.

So from now on you'll hear me exclaiming, "He's got this!" because Lord knows, I do not, my friend. Oh, how I do not.

We can be intentional about carving out moments in our day to remind us of our need for Him. We don't have to (and shouldn't) hold off until the eleventh hour to call in for backup. We can take moments to check in with God in the afternoon. Or at night. Or even right now!

Whenever you can carve out some time, do it and watch as it transforms the way you think about everything. As it turns out, no matter what your mommy plan looks like, you need Him holding your hand every step of the way. Sometimes all you need in life is to sit back and take a sip on a cup of He's Got This.

CHEERS TO ...

- Starting the process of releasing yourself from the paralyzing fears that come with the territory of being a momma.
- Avoiding the temptation to Google the answers to your questions rather than diving into God's Word.
- Acknowledging the areas you can control and giving the ones you can't to your Savior.
- Teaching your little ones that God will take care of them and will direct their paths, regardless of what Google has to say about it.
- And, last, to the fact that you can train yourself to do a whole lot of trusting and a lot less nail biting. #LetGoAndLetGod
- Today's Celebration: Discuss your motherhood fears with your spouse, your best friend, or whomever makes you most comfortable. Don't forget to discuss them with God as well. Maybe even jot them down in a journal to glance back at over time to see how God answers your prayers and relieves you of your worries. And then promise me,

and yourself, that over time you will release the straps to those backpacks full of worries and walk in faith clinging to this truth:

"For I know the plans I have for you," declares the LORD, "plans to prosper you and not to harm you, plans to give you hope and a future" (Jeremiah 29:11).

PART VIII

Squashing the Scheduling Savages

Mom Confession: My calendar is booked for the next eighteen years, and I'm in my feelings about it. Is it just me or does it seem like military operatives would be more manageable than motherhood at times?

CHEERS TO ...

TRUTH #8 – In Christ You Can Find Rest from the Parenting Rat Race

There are 168 hours in each week. Focus on the ones you will devote to God's kingdom, and the rest of your schedule will fall into place.

....

"Come to me, all you who are weary and burdened,
and I will give you rest. Take my yoke upon you
and learn from me, for I am gentle and humble in heart,
and you will find rest for your souls.
For my yoke is easy and my burden is light."

MATTHEW 11:28–30

21

The Solution to Stress-Gate

The other day, I read an article in a local magazine in which the author had interviewed six women about their morning routines. I can only assume she did not select *me* for this exercise because she knew I would not be awake and/or possess the get-up-and-do-it-ness required for this type of interview, *but whatever*.

Anyway, she spoke with a delightful woman who shared that she, like most moms, needs a little extra motivation to wake in the morning. She sets her alarm for a little after 4:00 a.m. each morning. Side Note: No. Just no. There is not one human being outside maybe a policeman or brain surgeon who requires such an early wake-up call, but this lady is doing things, y'all. Thus, she needs a little extra motivation in the morning.

I kid you not, she went on to share that when her alarm sounds, it is accompanied by a text message that reads "Beyoncé would get up." Now friends, I am not suggesting we idolize anyone in pop culture, but Beyoncé went from having her mother sewing her costumes in their own living room, to being a multibillion-dollar mogul. So all of that to say, if you need extra motivation too, there is no shame in the game, girlfriend.

Maybe for you it's Mother Teresa. For me personally, it's John Stamos. If I read a text in the morning that told me John Stamos wanted me to get up, well honey, I'd be showered and out the door in under twenty. Disclaimer: My husband is well aware of my John Stamos "thing," and we are working through it. We all have our sin, folks. #FixItJesus. All sass aside, we must cling to the motivators, whatever or whomever they may be, and put our noses to the grind.

But it's overwhelming. I get it.

Sometimes I dream that the calendar on my refrigerator is a monster hiding in my closet waiting until I fall asleep to pounce on my bed and devour me. Weird, I know. But I battle with that schedule week in and week out. Life can get *crazy* busy.

Each morning our bodies grow tense approximately thirty minutes before the alarm sounds or the first child signals the arrival of a new day. It's as if there's some kind of internal warning attempting to rescue us from the impending chaos: Don't do it. Get out of here. *Run!*

Then, without fail, it *does* happen. The sun wakes—as do the babies. Diapers must be changed, coffee must be made, backpacks/lunchboxes packed, and just when we think we've caught a five-minute window for a break in our favorite spot, it's out the door and into the world of insanity all over again.

As parents, we feel like taxi drivers enslaved to the daily grind. Mom Uber, if you will. From now on, let's refer to ourselves as child chauffeurs. Has a nicer ring to it, don't ya think? Our daily agendas read like army reconnaissance operatives consisting of seventy-five-plus activities to be completed before mid-morning snack: ballet, soccer practice, playdates, doctor visits.

Then, after conquering our to-do lists, we arrive back to the homestead to the unsettling fact that dinner remains on the agenda. *Dinner?!* Dun. Dun. Dun. Who in the world has the time to create new and exciting (and healthy, of course) menu plans each week? Even if we do sit down and design a Pinterest-worthy meal plan, somebody's not gonna be up for Grandma's Chicken and Rice Bake for the fourth week in a row. (Don't sweat it though, girl. I've got you covered in the next chapter.)

Next, we are greeted with rows of laundry baskets. Ladies, let me just say, with all the piles of laundry I do each week, I am now convinced there is a sweet family residing in my basement that I have not had the pleasure of meeting yet.

We feel like the weight of the world is resting on our overtired shoulders. If we can't attend to every item on the calendar for the week, we are a failure. Or so it seems. And it doesn't stop with the regular chaos associated with raising kids. Why is it that the second we have children, everybody and their brother decides we'd be the *perfect* candidate to coach a team, serve on a board, teach a Sunday school class, organize carpool, chaperone a field trip, host a baby shower, and the list goes on and on?

Is this some form of universal punishment for all those lazy college afternoons when our greatest worry was making it to a three-o'clock afternoon class all the way across campus two buildings down from our dorm?

Nowadays, even pharmaceutical companies are reminding moms that we "don't get sick days." The pressure is mounting. The calendar is so full, we couldn't read the plans for Monday if somebody paid us. We feel trapped in this vortex of appointments, calendar reminders, and obligations. The toilets haven't been scrubbed in weeks. The bed sheets are creating homes for crayons and Barbie shoes. There's never enough time to get it all done. So what happens, friends? *Something* or *someone* starts suffering.

To maintain our crazy-busy lives, we are forced to pick sides and make sacrifices. We develop our adult priority list. It's as if we design a point structure and start assigning values to each of our tasks:

Super Urgent.
Urgent.
Kinda Urgent.
Not So Urgent.
Who Cares?

Disappointment begins to rear its ugly head. Friends are let down when we repeatedly cancel plans with them. The church is frustrated when, for some reason, we *don't* feel up to volunteering for nursery since we already hang out with children for a living. There's little stressful savages lurking around each corner, just waiting for the chance to steal our joy. Just as we reach to put a checkmark next to each item on our to-do list (and oh how over-the-moon satisfying that truly is), a whole new list of expectations creeps up, as if out of thin air.

We feel pressured to keep up. Stay ahead, in charge, and on point at all times. We feel pressured to look a certain way. Act a certain way. Speak a certain way. And if that's not enough, we also feel the pressure to not visibly show just how much pressure we are under. We can't be the first one to crack. Oh no. No time for breakdowns. No time for time-outs. No time for *sanity.*

Ugh. Save that pressure for the slow-cooker, ladies! It's high time we just said no, friends. You know what all this pressure *really* is? You know who's at the helm of all this confusion, all this frustration, and all this mind-numbing, soul-crushing stress. You guessed it—the dirty little devil.

He wants nothing more than for us to spin a web of misery with our efforts to keep up. He loves seeing us cry ourselves to sleep when we just don't feel up to the challenge or when we experience defeat in daily mom life. It's this misguided belief that if we just keep up this intimidating, intense lifestyle that at some point we will feel rested and the days will get shorter. That the kids will be happier and somehow our marriages will become great again.

Front-Page News: Not. Gonna. Happen.

There's no amount of marathons we could run, PTO groups we could chair, ballet recitals we could attend, Barefoot-Contessa-approved brunches we could host, or Bible studies we could lead that would make God love us more than He already does. Whew. I feel better already. *How about you?*

It seems like there are several camps of us Momma Overachievers: (1) the Award-Seekers, (2) the Anti-Idle-Timers, and (3) the Busybodies. I invite you to find your camp and free yourself of the propaganda your party subscribes to.

Dear Award-Seekers,

We don't serve a God focused on checklists commanding us to meet these unrealistic demands of the daily grind. If we're just going at this life for some kind of medal, award, or recognition for "Most Involved," "Most Active," "Best Agenda Arranger," or "Momma-Who-Looks-Best-In-Her-Yoga-Pants-While-Running-Around-Like-A-Blubbering-Idiot," well, we might as well take a bow and turn out the lights, because that show is over. God isn't prepping any awards with those titles. Worthy of noting, to date there are no Olympic sports revolving around who has the cleanest entryway. Let's keep it that way, pretty please?

Dear Anti-Idle-Timers,

I get it. Your momma kept you busy and always on the run as a child. You have this innate urge to hop to the next activity. If your hands aren't busy or your brain overworking, it just doesn't seem right. It's the guilt trip, isn't it? If we falsely believe that idle time is "wasted" time, we should remind ourselves that even *God* rested on the seventh day.

Dear Busybodies,

Some of you can't help yourselves. This we know. There's some overactive gene running wild inside that pretty little head of yours and there's just nothing you can do about it. I commit to pray for you. But for those of us who have no excuses other than boredom, let's get it under control. Let's sit and be still. Let's be reminded of God's instruction, "Be still, and know that I am God" (Psalm 46:10).

And check this one out: "'The LORD will fight for you; you need only be still'" (Exodus 14:14).

We only get one chance at life (#YOLO). Do you want the pages of your memoir to be filled with anecdotes about how you always folded the laundry as soon as the buzzer went off and never left a crumb on the kitchen floor for longer than twenty seconds? Or do you want it spilling over with mentions of how you always snuggled your babies, served others, and made time to honor and worship God?

You may think that right now would be the perfect opportunity for me to pop in some kitschy advice like "Get up an hour earlier than your children and nail that to-do list, girl!" but I'm not going to do that because, as we already know by now, I have never done that once in my life, and I have no experience with the magical wonders that allegedly reside in that no-man's-land time of day.

What I *will* tell you is to find your margin moments. Find those almost shockingly quiet moments when your life is eerily still and get 'er done, girl. Your margin moment might pop up for you at a red light or at 4:00 a.m. when your baby is doing tummy time. These unicorn moments show up when we least expect them, and it's like the "Warm Donuts" sign at your local Krispy Kreme. You gotta snag 'em while they're hot!

Remind yourself in those margin moments that you are still *not* going to be able to check *every* single thing off the to-do list. Because "here's the thing about doing it all: even if you can do it all, no one can do it all well."[20] *Can I get an amen?!* Thank God that the whole world's issues are not resting on our shoulders alone. What an incredible encouragement coupled with a huge burden-lifter!

I don't think God is cool with our downtrodden demeanors when we succumb to the fact that we actually *can't* do it all. He's not going to stand idly by as we continue to feel engulfed by the world's pressures. He can't be down with us tossing even more on our proverbial plates.

....

When we say *no* or *not now* to stressors in our lives,
it automatically means that we are saying *yes* to
something or *someone* else.

....

Last week I reached my boiling point. I threw my hands in the air and waved 'em like I just didn't care. I did something that on the surface sounds like a stress-inducing nightmare, but, as I sit here sharing, I can assure you it was the *best* thing I've ever done for my family to date. I canceled *every single thing* on our agenda for three days. No school (let's be real—Mother's Day Out), no extracurricular activities, minimal cleaning, and minimal laundry. (Hey, we gotta have clean undies, folks.)

I have to let you in on the amazingness I found during that time. It was as if I had been whisked away to a Malibu treatment center and survived detox. It was a euphoria that I would give anything to recreate daily. But more than anything, my babies were ecstatic. They had one-on-one Mommy attention that they probably hadn't fully gotten since they were six months old.

We played. We built Lego towers and ceremoniously tore them down. We painted our toenails. We read every book on the book-shelf—*twice*. We splashed in recreational bath time. We giggled till we cried. And I have groundbreaking information to deliver: When we woke up the next day, the world was still turning, the house was still standing, no one called the FBI, and all the laundry baskets were still sitting outside the laundry room.

Turns out that dirty laundry *can't* hug you. Unswept floors *don't* talk back when you need a friend. The ironing board *doesn't* wish to spend hours bonding over conversation and fun outings. Your morning coffee mug *won't* play a monumental game of Eskimo kisses with you. Leaf-covered front porches *don't* seem to understand unconditional love.

But, quick reminder, kids DO. Kids *can* do all of those things and deserve *all* of those things from us too.

When we allow our mom tasks to overcome us, we may feel triumphant when the to-do list is happily ticked away, but what about our most important calling—mommyhood.

When we say *no* or *not now* to stressors in our lives, it automatically means that we are saying *yes* to something or *someone* else. When your child looks at your dirty laundry or dishes piling up in the sink, or maybe when they don't even realize there is any to be done, you know what he or she is really seeing? *"I am your priority, and you are focused on me."* I can tell you one thing for sure, I may not ever finish a load of laundry on the first try, but by goodness, I am not going to let a day go by without a snuggle session or two and a bucket full of giggles.

Our kids sense our priorities. Love is spelled T-I-M-E to them. Twenty years down the road, we won't regret that dress shirt we failed to perfectly iron, but we *will* lament over missed opportunities with our babies.

Obviously, we can't shut down the fort and call it a day for life. Oh, how I wish we could just snuggle these tiny gifts with no pressures of responsibility, but what we *can* do is remind ourselves that these precious lives have been entrusted to us. They are more important than any possible task we have jotted down in our monogrammed day planners. So let's be intentional about making *them* feel that way.

From now on, let's take back our lives, sit down for a minute, relax, take a nap, and how about this: let's open God's Word. And let's pray. Turns out we do have time for prayer no matter what, because God's phone lines are always open and He's listening 24/7/365.

What you do during the day really speaks to what you care about most. If you want to be on the cover of *Good Housekeeping* for having the most immaculate home of the year, then you probably need to disregard this chapter and stick to your militant cleaning schedule. *But* if you want to be accused of being the mom who loved her babies fiercer than you desired air to breathe, well, I've got a few ideas: Love Today. Laundry Tomorrow.

22

Move it, Mealtime MomBot!

You know that moment when it's five o'clock, the babies are screaming, the noodles are boiling over on the stove, the dog messed on the floor, and the doorbell is ringing all at the same time?

Yep. The days that make you want to pack a bag and board the next available flight to Never-Ever-Ever-Coming-Back-Land. Those moments are incredibly demoralizing; you feel all alone in this hellish reality, and there doesn't seem to be any escape routes.

Jesus. Take. The. Wheel.

Speaking of the worst days, were you aware, prior to giving birth, that meals, dinnertime, and food in general would become the bane of your existence? Did anyone ever warn you that it would require every ounce of your will to live to successfully feed your family three meals a day?

Because nobody cared to share that with me.

Cut to my kids being old enough for some "solid food." Okay, just typing that makes me shiver because now there's this whole *new* responsibility that I bear, and I hardly have enough time to flush after my one potty break of the day. Mom Confession: I got really bogged down with mealtime. Maybe you have too? I felt compelled to read every meal-planning article published in the last five years, buy all the "easy recipe" cookbooks (which, can I just make an announcement right now: Sausage Florentine atop poached eggs is not an easy recipe, folks), and even stalked food blogs, trying to learn how to be a better homemaker in the kitchen. All it got me was a whole new bucket of scheduling stress.

So today I am going to share with you what we do up in my house for mealtime. First, let me admit to you that I am not looking to win Organic Mother of the Year, so if you are looking for her, I apologize that someone misled you here. I would much rather order pizza and have the freedom to toss the plastic plates when we are done, head to the den, and play board games rather than be up all night scrubbing pots and pans after serving my kids a magazine-worthy meal that they could care less about. However, in all fairness, I don't want us eating junk every night either.

To that end, I sat down a few months ago to "meal plan"—otherwise known as this mythical activity wherein fairy godmothers dice and prep food, place said food in perfectly sized oven-safe containers, and warm it to perfection for their well-behaved lineage. However, you're not new here. So you know that I didn't *actually* do any of that. Instead, I sat down and made a theme night for each day of the week. (Are you now understanding the title of this book better?) I believe in celebrating everything, even mealtime on a Thursday. I hope that my approach to dinnertime doom will help you! I present to you my family's "meal plan":

Mondays = "Meat Monday"

Think spaghetti, hamburgers, steaks, or, frankly, whatever the butcher has so graciously prepackaged in the meat department that week. Throw in some sheet-pan-roasted veggies (with lots of balsamic, might I add), and you've got yourself a balanced meal.

Tuesdays = "Taco Tuesday"

Throw out some grilled chicken strips, shredded cheese, and salsa, and put a nice big check in the box for Tuesday, friend. Toss in a freshly ripe avocado just to enhance your awesomeness and please the food police. Also, what kid (or adult) doesn't love a glorified cheese-dip party? Serious question. If you are out there, please allow me to school you on living the good life, you poor unfortunate soul.

Wednesdays = "Whatever Daddy Brings Home Wednesday"

You got it, girl. This is takeout night at our house. I find giving myself that much-needed break in the middle of the week is just what my soul needs. It's like a national holiday plopped right there on Hump Day.

Thursdays = "Surf 'n' Turf It Up Thursday"

On Thursdays in my home, you will be served something delightful from Nemo's home base: shrimp, fish, or—heck, if I'm feeling fancy—you might even find a crab cake on your plate. You're welcome. Side Note: The "turf" portion of that title is so that Mommy doesn't feel bad when an angus beef hot dog or heaping helping of my latest insanely comforting casserole (#SouthernLife, y'all) ends up being served on those extra-tough Thursdays—because #SurvivalMode.

Fridays = "Pizza and Popcorn Party"

Time to celebrate again, friends. We made it another week! And this is me openly admitting that I serve my kids pizza *and* popcorn in the same meal. And no, I do not *always* stock up on pesticide-free veggies and make it from scratch in my brick oven. *Sue me.* I've got Papa John's on speed dial, and on those extra-stressful weeks, those guys are momma's best friends. That reminds me, I've been meaning to get with them about faster routes directly to my front door.

You get the idea, right? Slay the scheduling savage, do away with the dinner demons, and live your best *sane* life. It's in those moments when we don't have a clue what's for dinner (and couldn't care less) that we just need to take a step back from the situation, get our composure, and scream out to Jesus to come take over! If we try to take care of all the details and manage all the moving parts on our own, we will often fail. It's life. But with God, even our worst days seem more manageable because we have Him to lean on.

God knows the details of every one of our days before we even live them. Isn't that a reassuring truth? We know that before our feet touch the bedroom floor in the morning, God already has an agenda laid out for the day. He knows what we will wear, where we will go, and, *yep*, even what we are going to serve for dinner that night. He already knows the noodles will boil over and the babies will scream. If we just ask Him for guidance, He will get us through all of it.

Before I even turn to get out of bed each morning, I say (sometimes loudly), "Jesus, take the wheel," because I know from experience, by giving Him control of my day from the start, I'm already prepping for the highs *and* the lows. I am saying, "Jesus, walk by me every step of the way." And that's better than any meal prep could be anyway.

I encourage you to take a few minutes and read Psalm 139:1–18 with me today. Allow the words to comfort you and empower you with the knowledge that Jesus is all-knowing and *always* there. Then consider praying this prayer each morning, asking Jesus to take the wheel of your life: "Search me, God, and know my heart; test me and know my anxious thoughts [like, when will I have time to potty again?]. See if there is any offensive way in me [like, rage about what we're having for dinner], and lead me in the way everlasting" (Psalm 139:23–24).

Jesus. Take. The. Wheel.

23

Stepping Off the Struggle Bus: Prioritize Your Pandemonium

One of my *least* favorite things to do in all of mothering, is waking up my tiny ones for school in the morning. Now listen, I realize some of you just slung this book against the wall because you are accustomed to graveyard hours up in your house. I totally get it. On *all* other days (mainly Saturdays, when Mommy desperately needs that extra thirty minutes of sleep), my kids wake with the sun, but on school days, those little munchkins want to soak up some extra beauty sleep like they are Mia Thermopolis, Princess of Genovia.

After I've tiptoed around the house attempting to check nineteen things off the to-do list before havoc ensues (Who am I even kidding? When I've hit snooze for the thirtieth time in a row), the time comes when I must wake their tiny souls. So I creep in there and just stare for a minute at their little bodies curled around a pillow with slobber dripping down their chins, and I'm in awe. Sleeping babies are my all-time fave.

As soon as they feel me stalking them, they open those little eyes and off we go into the land of insanity. "Take your pajamas off!" "Brush your teeth!" "Get your Barbie out of the microwave, Annalise!" The morning time hustle is so real.

And there are lots of things in life that require hustle. Fortunately, we never have to hustle for God's love and acceptance. He died on a cross, covered our transgressions with His blood, and extends infallible grace to us each and every day.

One reason we can't seem to grasp God's love, is we have never experienced anything even close to it here on this earth. Think of the relationship in your life today that brings you the most peace, satisfaction, joy, and acceptance. That's not even close to how much God loves you!

God wants the best for us in all situations (Romans 8:28). He would never want to see us resort to Ambien or coffee addictions just to survive the daily grind. He wants to provide us with opportunities that will foster lifelong relationships, give us chances to display our spiritual gifts, and afford us contagious joy.

Maybe it's time we had a DTR ("define the relationship") with each item on our agenda: Are we idolizing certain tasks? Are we exalting something or someone to the throne of our hearts that doesn't deserve that designation? We probably shouldn't complain that we don't have time for God if we're filling each weeknight with Netflix binge sessions, *Bachelor* viewing parties, or embarrassingly long Facebook stalking activities—food for thought.

He's probably staring at us right now, thinking, *Gee, I sure wish you'd take a few minutes each day to remember me. You do remember me, right? The One who created you? The One who saved you? The One who loves you beyond imagination? It's me. I'm still here. I wish you jotted my name on the calendar like you do yoga or CrossFit or Mommy and Me Gymnastics.*

Ouch.

God's right though. Somehow, on these password-protected, guarded-by-robot schedules we're all adhering to, there never seems to be an entry labeled "God-time." Maybe, *just maybe*, that's the source of all our problems. Could it be that we are focusing on everything *but* the most important thing? Have we forgotten our Main Man? Have we put God in a corner? *Gasp!*

When we consider our lives in the "hindsight is 20/20" context, it puts things into perspective. Is it *really* going to matter how many Capri Suns we handed out at soccer matches or cookies we baked for PTO meetings? Chances are, probably not. We might be considered earthly super moms, but if we know that only what we do for God will last, it sure does serve to refocus our efforts.

....

There are seven days in each week. It just so happens that "someday" isn't one of the days.

....

The phrase "I just don't have time" creeps up a lot in life, doesn't it? Often, we insert that age-old response when we just really don't want to do whatever it is we are being propositioned to do. There's a big difference in saying "I can't" and "I choose not to because it's not a priority of mine." It's important for us to become a little more intentional about how we respond to requests made by others. Since at the end of the day, it's not about *having* time, it's really about *making* time for what's important. As it turns out, there are seven days in each week. It just so happens that "someday" isn't one of the days.

I've heard it said that actions express priorities. In order to discover what ours are, let's look at where we spend our time and talents. Our priorities are *not* what we claim them to be; they are visible by the way we choose to live our lives.

So, friend, what are *your* priorities? Who and what *really* matter to you? What items on your agenda are non-negotiables, meaning those items you are going to honor no matter the sacrifice required? Quick Test: Grab a pen and a piece of paper, and honestly answer the following questions. (The wadded-up napkin lying next to you on the couch will be just fine. At least, that's what I found close by.)

1. *Who* do you spend most of your time with? Your kids? Your spouse? Your friends? Your computer? Your cell phone?

2. *What* would you do if you had a free day with no obligations? (Spoiler Alert: It's perfectly okay to answer "spa day" here. I did.)

3. *When* do you fit God into your agenda? Does He often get forgotten in the daily grind?

4. *Where* do you spend most of your time during the week? Why?

5. *How* much do you care about the label on the tag inside your shirt right now, how your hair looks, or what kind of car you drive?

6. *Why* do you say yes to certain activities and no to others. Our whys in life happen to be pretty significant triggers for understanding our deepest motivations.

Okay, whew! I was told there would be no incessant questioning.

Now that we have a better, more transparent view of our hearts, we can focus on what God tells us about our priorities and motivations in life.

In this crazy-busy life we each lead, we need to set aside certain aspects that are non-negotiable priorities. We need to be protective and ensure that we make time and reserve resources for *those* priorities. The Bible provides some guidance for us on this very topic. From what I gather, there are five purposeful priorities we should strive to possess in our lives:

Faith

"But seek first the kingdom of God and His righteousness." (Matthew 6:33)

There doesn't seem to be any question that our relationship with the Lord should be our number-one priority in life. This includes striving to follow Christ's leadership, attending regular worship, serving others, tithing, reading God's Word regularly, spending time in prayer, and living with an attitude of gratefulness. When we put

Him first, everything else (even Mommy and Me Zumba) will some-how always fall into place.

Family

> For if someone does not know how to manage his own house-hold, how will he care for God's church? (1 Timothy 3:5 ESV)

God's greatest gifts to us (next to salvation, of course) are our family members. These individuals have been hand-picked by God and placed in our lives. Whoa. That kinda gives me chills thinking about it like that! Time spent with your loved ones is never wasted. No matter how busy life gets, I can promise you that you will never regret carving out time for your favorite peeps. But kids and their schedules can present some of the toughest items to juggle on the agenda. Real Talk: God is the captain of our ships. As the mommas, we get to play the role of cruise director. God will always be the One steering (thank the good Lord!), but we have the opportunity to manage those schedules, edit them where necessary, and take care of business. There's yet another way to get the schedule back in check!

Function

> "But I have raised you up for this very purpose, that I might show you my power and that my name might be proclaimed in all the earth." (Exodus 9:16)

What has God designed you to do? Other than be an awesome mom, of course. What burning desires do you have in your heart that maybe even keep you up at night? You have a calling, girl. Maybe even lots of them. And God expects you to tend to those talents He's so graciously hooked you up with. I'll tell you one function you most definitely have: share the love of Christ. Only what's done for Christ will last anyway. So start today. Don't wait for others to share the love. Show them how.

Friendship

Be devoted to one another in love. Honor one another above yourselves. (Romans 12:10)

You know how I feel about tappin' your tribe by now. I can go ahead and promise you that there will be days you will need your friends more than anything else on the planet. Because outside our families, our friends are the closest ones to our hearts. They are those special little people whom God plops right along our journeys of life to make it a little bit easier and a whole lot more fun. Making your friends a priority isn't just a blessing to them; it will be a mega-blessing for you too!

Fitness

"Do you not know that your bodies are temples of the Holy Spirit, who is in you, whom you have received from God? You are not your own; you were bought at a price. Therefore honor God with your bodies." (1 Corinthians 6:19–20)

No, I am not suggesting you rush out and join a gym, *although* physical fitness is super important too. I'm talking about your faith fitness. You may be thinking, *But we just discussed faith in number one, right?* Yes. But faith fitness is something more specific. It's about making sure that this vessel God blessed you with—your earthly body—is always in tip-top shape.

While you can certainly add some cardio to your week, also be mindful about what you put inside your body (what you view on TV, the kind of music you listen to, and the places you go). This is all about being mindful about what the world (and especially our little ones) hear us saying, see us doing, and watch us focusing on.

As a bonus, for those who, like me, want to have a little fun in life, God speaks to that as well: "I have come that they may have life, and have it to the full" (John 10:10).

As you reflect on your priorities, pray that God will show you exactly how to adjust your priorities to travel closer and closer to the center of His will. Create a purposeful priorities list and remain dedicated to living out your faith on a daily basis, no matter how crazy busy this life tends to get.

24

Pouty Lips and Pedicures

The second we have children, we lose one of the most time-honored privileges: peeing alone. Yup. Forget about ever sneaking away to the potty for a minute to yourself. In fact, if you ever lose one of your kids inside your house one day, just walk in the general direction of the bathroom. I promise you they will show up before you flush.

The first week after my youngest started Mother's Day Out, her teacher called me and said she needed to "fill me in on some things." Of course, I bit my entire bottom lip off in fear that my child had spit in some kid's face or "added to the beauty" of another kid's artwork by splattering her red-marker details right in the middle of it.

Thank God it was neither of those. Instead, her teacher informed me that every time my tot needed to potty, she turned to the teacher and said, "Excuse me. I will need some privacy, lady." Her teacher informed me that this was cute. I informed her that this phrase was used every single time I needed to go to the restroom at home; it was a learned behavior; and that this was not cute, it was called survival. And I kindly asked her to inform my precious and seemingly modest tot, that yes, she would indeed be permitted privacy, so long as she afforded it to her loved ones at home as well.

We lose privacy, we lose sleep, and we definitely lose sanity when our babies arrive. I'm not going to lie to you; we're all friends here. I fell asleep on my toddler as Bob and Larry blasted VeggieTales showtunes in the background this past weekend. Plus, I really wish you could see the super-attractive streak of gray hair blossoming above my right eye with reckless abandon, as it has not seen my hair stylist in months.

My husband ~~lovingly~~ sneakily captured the moment with his cell phone to show me why I so desperately needed to "get out more" and partake in some mommy time-outs. Despite the snuggle-bunny dreams you may have conjured up while envisioning me snoozing on my tiny tot, that moment was the perfect depiction of a worn-out soul whose last iota of will to go on finally gave up on her. If I hadn't taken a chill moment right after, you would have found me in the local TJ Maxx, hunting for my insane-asylum prom dress right about now.

Are you feeling overwhelmed today? Overworked? Undervalued? Do you feel like the weight of the world is on your shoulders and no one is there to lighten your load? Are you staring at your calendar and realizing that if you try to fit one more thing in your brain, it will most likely explode or, possibly even worse, shut down?

Maybe you are in the same boat (or bus) that I am. You've given it all you've got, you've signed up for every PTA activity, you've attended every playdate, changed every diaper, washed every load of clothes, and you're—just—tired. You've had it with reality. Even propping your eyelids open with toothpicks isn't an option at this point. I feel you, sister.

Maybe you feel this way too: "Oh, I couldn't possibly take a moment to myself because my babies need me, my husband needs me, the church needs me, this house will implode, the spaghetti noodles won't get cooked, the towels won't get folded properly, the walls will cave in, and St. Peter will give up my spot in line if I take a—gasp—break!"

Well, I'm here to tell you, friends, as shocking as this may sound, life *will* go on—and maybe even a little better than it did before. It's time we all took a step (read: giant leap) off the struggle bus and sauntered into the Mommy-Minute Time-Out Park for a bit.

If we want to teach our children the importance of loving themselves and having self-worth, we must model it for them. If all they ever see is a haggard woman bent over at the kitchen sink barely getting by, that image will be burned in their brains forever. That, they will think, is what motherhood must really look like. On the other hand, if we make it a point to take a breather here and there, and—I don't know—maybe take a full shower, we are modeling for our children a woman who makes herself a priority too.

"There is no VIP section at the foot of the cross."[21] There are no rewards for the moms who slave away, never coming up for a breather, and suffer in silence. A little absence here and there truly does make the heart grow fonder. Our kids actually need breathers from us too. So if you refuse to think of yourself, think of them. They need a moment or two of "me" time too.

It is not selfish to take a breather. Not. N-O-T. I used to think that if I did anything whatsoever for myself, then I was robbing my babies of the unicorn-light-of-a-thousand-fairies dream existence that I so desperately want to afford them. What I didn't realize was that in my hollow attempts to be the "best mom," I was actually robbing myself and my babies of a great mom. Because, as it turns out, when we don't fill our own cups of goodness, we won't have anything to pour into the ones we love either.

No matter why any of us may be tired/down/discouraged today, it's time for us to ditch the pouty lips and indulge in a pedicure—even if that means locking ourselves in the bathroom for twenty minutes.

The key to overcoming the chaos of #MomLife is finding a way to replace that chaos with joy. Outside your babies, what brings you joy? What really makes you tick? For some, it might be a trip to the mall, taking a nap, or getting a massage. For others, it's a month-long trip in the Andes. For me, it was writing this book. Find that thing (or those things) that give you life and indulge them, schedule them, and don't feel bad for seeing to it that they get checked off the to-do list too.

Being a mom is a constant balancing act. We give all our attention to our little blessings, but at times that naturally causes us to feel lost in the shuffle. There's no longer time for long walks on the beach, binge-watching our favorite shows, and date night. Even going to the bathroom alone is a thing of the past!

But it doesn't have to be this way.

I realized not too long ago, a large part of the reason I never felt like I had time was actually my own fault. I'm a self-admitted control freak. Well, let me reterm myself. I am a self-admitted family manager. I want everything done correctly, timely, and efficiently, and when I say *correctly*, I mean to *my* standards. Anyone with me on this?

The only reason I'm able to admit that I am a control freak—um, family manager—is so that my beloved family members won't force me into expensive therapy only to realize months down the road that, yep, I'm a control freak—I mean, family manager. But you know what's cool? Now that I've admitted that I am one, I can control—that is, manage—my response to those overwhelming feelings that tend to creep up.

Part of my issue is this burdensome feeling that if I go into my bedroom and close the door, the house is somehow going to explode without my active presence. It's this gnawing fear that my temporary stepping away will be the trigger for chaos.

That's all in our heads, mommas. I have recently learned that stepping away for a few seconds is mandatory, in some cases, to *prevent* chaos.

So today I hope you feel encouraged and empowered because you deserve some "me" time and rest too. Jesus even instructed the apostles to rest: "Then, because so many people were coming and going that they did not even have a chance to eat, he said to them, 'Come with me by yourselves to a quiet place and get some rest'" (Mark 6:31).

Whoa. Didn't even have time to eat? Sound familiar, mommas?

Time-outs, playdates, naptimes, and even mealtimes don't have to be reserved just for the toddlers anymore.

We all need to REST:
R – Restore your soul.
E – Exalt God.
S – Serve others by filling up on His goodness.
T – Trust that God will always provide.

Just in case you weren't convinced to take some "me" time after learning that Jesus told the disciples to get some rest, Mark 4:38 tells us that even Jesus took a nap here and there too. Well, there it is, friends. Jesus took naps. Go and be like Jesus.

So today I am giving you, my newest mom-tribe member, an invitation to join me for a few mommy time-outs this week. We'll take it slow at first. You know, dipping our toes into the dewy goodness of the grass in Mommy Time-Out Park.

Take a walk.

Go buy the groceries—alone.

Lock yourself in the bathroom and read for thirty minutes.

For goodness sakes, take that much-needed nap you've been daydreaming about since your firstborn entered the world. You deserve it, and your precious family does too.

CHEERS TO ...

- 🦆 Acknowledging your triggers and need for rest.
- 🦆 Taking some "me" time this week to recharge.
- 🦆 Today's Celebration is three parts:
  1. Turn your phone off for one consecutive hour today. Promise me you won't even check to see if someone has texted or called during this window of time. We are starting with a manageable block of time and can always up it from here. Take this hour and do nothing but read, roll around on the floor, craft, and

play with your children. Ask your child what he or she would like to do. Maybe you could go to a park, the local zoo, or a museum. Make some memories. Invest in your children. Social media will be there when you get back. TV shows can be recorded. Now is the time to invest in your little ones and spend time on what matters most.

2. Take a minute and list your priorities. What are the focuses of your life? List all your activities and go through them one by one. Are they bringing you and your family joy? Are they furthering the kingdom? Are they necessary for survival? If you answered no to any of those questions, consider kicking some of those time fillers to the curb and dedicating your free moments to the ones that matter.

3. Schedule some "me" time. Every mom requires moments to themselves to recharge. It's so important—not just for yourself, but for your family as well. Make it a priority to carve out some time this week and read, craft, go to the mall, attend a concert, have a spa day, or just take a nap. Whatever you need to rejuvenate, do that and know that by doing so, you are doing what is best for your family too!

PART IX

Adulting: Accept the Challenge. Play by the Rules. Win at Parenting.

Mom Confession: I rocked it out at planning the baby registry, attending all the classes, and decorating the nursery, but the thought of teaching my children everything they need to know by the age of eighteen has me high-key stressing. Step 1. Birth baby. Step 2. Bring them home. Step 3. *Now what do I do?*

CHEERS TO ...

TRUTH #9 – You Know What's Up with This Whole Parenting Thing

As we are all now acutely aware, children are not born with instruction manuals strapped to their tiny ankles. But have no fear. The framework for parenting is found in God's Word.

....

If any of you lacks wisdom, you should ask God,
who gives generously to all without finding fault,
and it will be given to you.

JAMES 1:5

25

Fix It, Jesus!

'm looking for an "I see you, sister" moment today, friend. *Can you help me?*

The first seventy-two hours of Bellalise's life were some of the most amazing moments of my life. They were also, simultaneously, some of the scariest I can remember. Once I got the chance to hold my little one after spending ten months keeping her safe inside, I was immediately struck with over-the-moon awe coupled with complete and total hysteria.

I delivered her and there she was, this teeny thing, completely dependent on my ability to get it together and figure it all out. When the nurses rudely interrupted our skin-to-skin time (because, apparently, even newborns have modesty these days), my little girl said, "Oh heck no!" and demanded, through loud screams and out-stretched arms, to be placed back on my chest.

I live for a passionate woman, people. And *this* one was all mine. We didn't leave that passion in Brookwood Hospital's Room 311 though. Nope. We packed up all that passion and bravado, tucked it in our suitcases, and headed for home. That same passion and bravado pops up from time to time nowadays too. You know, like in the crowded local meat-and-three at lunchtime, or the Target dressing room, or, my personal favorite, in the quiet part of the offertory hymn during Sunday-morning church.

More than eighty million times in my parenting, I've looked up at God and screamed, "What the heck do I do now?!" I'd be lying if I didn't admit I ask that same question almost daily, but the urgency and cold-sweat nightmares have subsided, *for the most part*. Praise be.

As promised, I'm not about to teach you how to make your baby love kale (eww) or how to conduct themselves in public. I *am* going to share with you what God has taught me about *surviving* and maybe even *thriving* through all of it. First, I am going to point you to a reminder that I have scheduled to pop up on my phone at random times throughout the week: "Seek the LORD and his strength; seek his face continually" (1 Chronicles 16:11 KJV).

In the interest of full disclosure, my alerts simply say, "Fix it, Jesus," but you get my drift.

The specific date our children begin crawling, whether or not they enjoyed peas, and how tall they were as they entered kindergarten won't matter at the pearly gates. That's a real stop-you-in-your-tracks kind of moment, isn't it? Society trains us, *taunts us really*, to win all the mom awards by seeing to it that our children are exceeding and smashing through all the proverbial glass ceilings, but what about the milestones that *really* matter—the heart ones? The real question we should be asking ourselves is this: Are my children being fed the hope and grace of Christ?

··

When we feel like everything around us is falling apart, we are forced to come face-to-face with the only constant we have—Christ Himself.

··

One of my fondest memories from childhood involves me sneaking into our kitchen, once everyone was in bed, to steal sips of orange soda from the fridge. This hysteria-inducing sugar-booger was off limits to the youngsters in the Brown family home. My game of deceit provided me way too much joy, as I would return multiple times to the fridge just to see how many of them I could get away with. Side Note: I can't even fathom a repeat of my Sunkist story in today's society, since Sunkist is clearly *full* of high-fructose corn syrup—*ah, the good ole days!*

My life on the edge didn't stop with my penchant for diabetic-causing orange soda. I'm the kid who purposely placed my finger on the burning stove a total of ten seconds after my precious momma warned against such an activity. I'm also the kid who dumped an entire box of Cheerios on the floor so we would be late to church on multiple occasions— maybe you also remember all those fun facts about my rebelliousness I shared in chapter two. I'm a rebel without a cause despite the fact that my parents are literal rock stars at the whole parenting thing—until God rocked *my* world with two babies under two, and I imagine He chuckled as He asked me, "Now, what are you gonna do with *all of this?*"

Um, I'll take "Escape to a deserted island" for $200, Alex!

Sure, we can go out and buy all the parenting books available, read them, and apply each one of the million suggestions, but if we are not primarily pointing our babies to Christ, what's the point? We are often tempted to think that our "awesome" parenting tactics will automatically produce "awesome" kids. But "it's not ultimately a parent's *hard work* that produces the fruit of the Spirit in our children's lives; rather it's the Holy Spirit's *heart work.*"[22]

I want to adopt Paul's words as the mantra for my own parenting: "I have no greater joy than to hear that my children are walking in the truth" (3 John 1:4).

My momma didn't prevent me from drinking way too many Sunkists, but she pointed me to Christ. She couldn't stop me from burning my finger a time or two, but she stopped me from believing that my way was the *only* way.

I don't know about you, but the moments I have felt strongest in my life were the ones in which I was actually the weakest. When

I *didn't* have the answers and was often sitting there without a clue. That sounds backward, but when we are dealing with anything from a restaurant temper tantrum or a soda-sucking tot, all the way to an all-out crisis, *those* are the moments we see Christ's face so clearly. Those are the instances when He not-so-subtly reminds us that He *is* there. When we feel like everything around us is falling apart, we are forced to come face-to-face with the only constant we have—Christ Himself. He will never leave us and never forsake us, and He is there when everyone else has walked out. God uses our struggles to reinforce our necessity for Him.

This is my prayer for my babies:

> I pray that out of his glorious riches he may strengthen you with power through his Spirit in your inner being, so that Christ may dwell in your hearts through faith. And I pray that you, being rooted and established in love, may have power, together with all the Lord's holy people, to grasp how wide and long and high and deep is the love of Christ, and to know this love that surpasses knowledge—that you may be filled to the measure of all the fullness of God. (Ephesians 3:16–19)

In parenting, and in life, when you just don't have a clue, seek *His* face, friends. Seek. His. Face.

26

Pop Out Your Planners for the Parenting To-Do List

This may be surprising considering how put together and organized I must seem after getting this far in the book (tracking with my wit yet, y'all?), but true story: I thrive if I have a list, in almost every scenario life throws at me.

For example, if you send me into a grocery store *without* a list, you are going to be the lucky recipient of every single "new" item/ gimmick and hot-off-the-press Oreo flavor the store had to offer that day. You will also be forced to phone the FBI in an attempt to locate my whereabouts because, according to reports, I entered the Bermuda Triangle somewhere around aisle seven.

However, if you send me in there *with* a detailed list, you are going to ignite the momma-on-a-mission in me, my OCD will rear its ugly head, and I will view my grocery-shopping task as the newest sport in the Olympics, yielding us with a much more manageable bounty. Where my fellow list-loving girls at? I see you, sisters. Huddle up for all the love.

I truly wish God had drafted up a little *Girlfriend's Guide to Mommyhood* for us. I really, really do. But since He chose to omit that little ditty of a surefire best seller, I've spent an ungodly amount of time scouring what He and His co-contributors *did* say, to come up with what I am proud to report is a pretty manageable list for nailing this whole parenting thing.

I'm not going to lay out a three-step foolproof plan for parenting because (1) that would be laughable considering my babies are six and four at the time of this publication, meaning I'm right there with you in the grenade-filled ditch, sister; *and* (2) as if we haven't already beaten this dead horse enough, there are *no* perfect parenting plans.

However, I am *not* going to leave you hanging, because today I am sharing the seven things I think God's Word tells us about being good parents. Or at least the seven things God keeps reminding me at 1:00 a.m. on a Tuesday morning, when the rest of the people of the world are resting peacefully in their beds, enjoying their seventieth REM cycle, and I am searching for that (insert non-Sunday-school-appropriate word here) missing sock that fell off my child's foot for the thirty-four-billionth time in a row.

Here goes.

First: Get Pre-Prayed

> This is the confidence we have in approaching God: that if we ask anything according to his will, he hears us. (1 John 5:14)

When I was prepping for my newborn, I did all the things. I spent hours in baby stores selecting ridiculous items that no baby could ever possibly need. I read every book that presented itself in the parenting section at my local bookstore. I attended more parenting prep classes than I care to share with you at this time. I spent ten months of this child's life prepping her for the moment she would take her first breath. The moment, after which, every moment will follow for her "real-world life."

But it really hit me as I was lying in my hospital bed, preparing to give birth: Have I *pre-prayed* this child? Have I talked to God about her first day? Have I asked Him to guide her, shield her, and protect her? Have I given *Him* my anxiety? I had been so worried about selecting the perfect first-day outfit, packing all the pristine new baby things, and getting to the hospital in plenty of time, that I forgot to check the most important thing off my to do list—*pray*.

A few nights ago I was tucking my girls into bed, and I encouraged them to say their night-night prayers. My oldest said, "Mommy, I want to pray for *all* my people." It sounds so simple, but it made such an impact on me. Do we stop and pray for "all our people" every day? Do we give God even the smallest things?

At times, we save prayer for the really big stuff like when someone loses their job or a health crisis hits, but I want you to know that yours truly is praying about runny noses just as much as I'm praying about running ragged after a long day of mommin'. Maybe it's high time we checked in with our most important tribe member.

There are few things in life more comforting than a good catch-up session with a dear friend. Due to life's crazy schedules, distractions, and distance, sometimes friendships get shelved for periods of time. We tend to put off visiting with one another to make room for other more-pressing agenda fillers. Sometimes we do that with God too. We sort of "shelve" Him until we have a few minutes left at the end of the day. After we've watched all our TV, caught up for hours on social media, finished the laundry, done the dishes, and packed all the lunches. But He never shelves us. He never puts us on a to-do list for later. He's available to us 24/7/365. He doesn't take holidays. He doesn't have sick days. He never heads out on vacay. He is everywhere we go.

Driving down the interstate a few years ago, I noticed a massive billboard in the distance. I could barely read the font until I got closer, but when I did, it changed the way I thought about prayer. The billboard read "God is *everywhere*, so pray *anywhere*."

Doesn't that thought generate all the feels? Rather than looking at prayer as an item to add to the daily to-do list, let's start looking at it as an open invitation to talk to our Savior! We can talk to Him while we fold the laundry. We can chat while we shower and change. We can holler out for God's healing when we stub our toe, for goodness sakes!

I find that if I spend even ten minutes in uninterrupted conversation with God, He jolts me back into shape. He takes that wheel like nobody else, even sweet little Carrie Underwood. He points out areas where I need to improve and shows me how I can trust in Him to get it done. If you don't have time for a full devotional right now (I totally get it! #Solidarity), then maybe consider downloading a quick app such as the *First 5* app. Every morning or night, open it up, read the passage for the day, and just pray. Preserve that time every day for you and God. If we've got time for playdates and/or Mommy and Me Pedicures, we certainly have time for our Savior. You'll definitely find *me* praying these days.

Next time you see me with my head bowed in carpool line, don't fret. I've either dozed off (thank God for carpool-pick-up-line naps!) or, more likely, I'm in a deep convo with the Lord "pre-prayering" my kiddos and myself for all our days. "And pray in the Spirit on all occasions with all kinds of prayers and requests" (Ephesians 6:18).

Second: Kick Negative Nelly to the Curb and Hang Out More with Merry Sunshine

> Give thanks to the LORD, for he is good; his love endures forever. (Psalm 118:1)

There are a whole lot of days when the last thing on my mind is thanking God for my screaming toddlers. But, Lord, am I thankful God chose me to love on these little blessings. When I think about all the alternatives, all the *other* paths my life could have taken, I am eternally grateful that God tapped me for this day, this hour, *for such a time as this.* He doesn't make mistakes. He has provided us a calling. Let's thank Him for it.

Oh, and Spoiler Alert: Your girl up the street with the perfectly coifed children—the one who dishes out dinners that would make Rachael Ray look like a soup-kitchen volunteer—is walking down the exact same path you are. She may make it look a little more aesthetically pleasing than others, but there are Barbie heads hiding somewhere up in her couch too. #Truth.

So be thankful for the flowers growing in your garden, even the wilting roses with spiky thorns, because there's beauty there too, if only we look for it.

God didn't promise us life would be easy and pretty and Pinterest-perfect. Actually, He told us it would be hard and messy and even ugly at times. So if we are going to soak up all the beautiful life-giving moments, we have to be thankful for those tough ones too. It is in *those* moments that Christ is shaping us and bringing us back to Him.

Third: Tune in to TV's Latest Hit: Grace and ~~Frankie~~ Your Babies

> Let us then approach God's throne of grace with confidence, so that we may receive mercy and find grace to help us in our time of need. (Hebrews 4:16)

Did you wake up today? High-five! It appears you did. Did you get breakfast today? If you did, that is so awesome! If not, insert an imaginary chest bump here, because I'm over here jonesin' for my next meal too. Did you get to take a shower—uninterrupted … yet? If you did, I am unashamedly so jealous of you right now. But also, hey, can you send me a quick email with some secrets to achieving that feat? I've got two kids. Get creative. Thanks! Have you finished all your laundry yet? Girrrrl, just kidding! I'm serving mine for dinner tonight in the form of baskets to be folded. Laundry is for overachievers, am I right?

If we fret about all the things I just mentioned, we are subconsciously teaching our babies that we've got to have it all together and be all things to all people. But we know the Bible teaches us that He gives grace—*abundantly*. Our weaknesses expose God's strength. "Bad days do not make bad moms."[23] "God wants us to know His joy when we have good days and wants us to experience His grace when we don't."[24]

Grace is God's way of opening His arms up wide to us, when we get it right and even when we don't. So let's take a minute each day to remind ourselves that it's more important to get and give grace than it is to get it all right.

Fourth: Take a Cue from Rascal Flatts and Be All about Blessin' Those Broken Roads

> Let us not become weary in doing good, for at the proper time we will reap a harvest if we do not give up. (Galatians 6:9)

I wish I could say "push through the rough days" and be done with it, but we all know it's not that easy. Life is going to outright blow at times. Admitting it is the first step.

It used to really tick me off when people would say, "Parenting is a marathon, not a sprint!" Yeah, girl, we know. Oh, how we know. Then I realized there's a whole lot of hope in that catchy little phrase. We *don't* have to get it all right today. Or tomorrow. We just have to survive today to *get* to tomorrow. Each night we can quickly re-evaluate what went well today and what *didn't* go so well. Once we see areas of improvement, we can switch it up to make things better for the next day. Maybe we need to put our cell phone down more. Maybe we need to remember to take a ten-minute break every hour. Or maybe we need to seek a little outside help. No matter what, being self-aware, recognizing areas of improvement, and committing to do better tomorrow is really all we can do, friends.

Now that we know every day is not going to be the best day ever, we can temper our expectations and cling to the hope of a better tomorrow because, God willing, the sun *will* set on those hellish days, and the sun *will* rise on fresh opportunities to get it a little closer to being "right." To be a little more patient. To give a little more grace. And to hold on to Christ a little bit tighter.

Fifth: Be a Good Monkey

In everything set them an example by doing what is good [Note: Paul did not say *perfect* here]. (Titus 2:7)

Our former pastor, Dr. Gary Fenton, performs the most beautiful *and* meaningful baby dedications. He personalizes them to each family. More importantly, he takes that moment in time to truly speak to the parents and the church about their responsibilities in the child's life. As he gazes into the child's eyes, he suddenly shifts his focus to the parents and softly speaks these words: "This child will occasionally listen to you, but she will *always* be watching you."

Wow. Let the truth of that simple statement sink in for a moment. What a powerful reminder!

As moms, we can relentlessly search the internet for the answers to being the "best mom." The truth is actually much simpler to discover than all the hassle we exert. "Monkey see, monkey do." We've heard that catchy little phrase our whole lives, but now that bad boy is all too real for the momma tribe. Does anyone else feel like we are each starring in our own little season of *Big Brother*, and we've surrendered the privilege of stealing away to pick our nose in privacy from now until eternity? Ah, the perks of singledom.

Our little ones stare at us with laser-like accuracy, and while they may never listen to us explaining proper potty etiquette, they will *always* catch us slipping a curse word when we drop the laundry basket on our feet.

While we know perfect behavior is an impossible standard we shouldn't even aspire to, we've got to be the light more times than not. We've got to raise them up to know that even when we make mistakes, we are striving to do what is right.

If you wish for your children to be *kind*, be kind to others. Even when you're tired. Even when the cashier is making you angry. Even when someone slams on their brakes in front of you, causing you to veer off the road. Strive to teach your children that you cannot control other's actions, you can only control your own actions and your own reactions. Even when you want to react so hard to Facebook Frieda and her fingernail comment, you know you better not—this time anyway. You've got this, girl. You can rise above!

If you wish for your children to be *grateful*, say thank you in front of them. Thank the fast-food cashier. Thank your kids when they clean their rooms, wash their hands, and share with others. Thank the librarian. Heck, thank everybody! Show them how to thank God for their food, their clothes, and their health. Side note: *Jesus, be a clean floor, tidy potty, and on-time dinner peeps.*

If you wish for your children to be *patient*, hold yourself back from going one to one hundred in under five seconds when they just can't seem to get it together at 7:15 a.m. As a fellow morning avoider, may I plead on their behalf for a moment? The morning time struggle is, honestly, so real, guys. Give them the extra five minutes to tie their shoes properly (even when you needed to be out the door ten minutes ago). Offer them grace (even in the moments that send you straight to the insane asylum), because God offers you undeserved, indescribable amounts of grace, even on your worst days too.

If you wish for your children to be *truthful*, tell the truth. Even little white lies are easily exposed by our super-sleuth kiddos. Track with this instead: If you say you will take your kiddos to a friend's house for a playdate, you might better plan on making good on that promise. Promises to children are life-and-death. When you utter the words "I will," "We will," or any version of "I promise," remind yourself that you have just entered into a binding oral contract with your little ones, and as an attorney, I can conclusively report to you that there is no contract more binding than the one you just made with your two-year-old this morning.

If you wish for your children to be *giving*, be charitable with the many blessings God has given you. Take opportunities to expose your kids to the power of sharing their time and talents. Take a Saturday to clean out your closets and donate the clothing to a local women's shelter or church. Be part of a toy or school supply collection that benefits local children in need. Stop by a nursing home to minister to residents. Take a meal to a friend.

If you wish for your children to be *responsible*, follow through with your own commitments. If you take on a role at work, school, or church, commit to serving in the best capacity possible. This may require making sacrifices like wiping other kids' bottoms in the nursery at church, even though you can think of 1.6 million other things you'd rather be doing. The example you will be setting for your children is by far worth the extra effort and icky diaper-pail moments any day.

I could go on and on—the list of cause-and-effect parenting rules is endless—but we get the idea. "The proof is in the pudding," as we've heard it said so many times before. Sometimes it's easy to let ourselves slack in terms of being kind, grateful, patient, truthful, giving, and responsible, when we are only exercising those traits for ourselves. And truth be told, there is *no way* for any of us to be perfect all the time. Perfect behavior is a losing game, my friends. (Thank goodness!) But when we look at it through the lens of a parent showcasing proper behavior in front of our child, it will shift our focus.

Children will emulate celebrities, musicians, and even popular Olympians today, but the humbling fact remains that the people they *should* be looking up to most are their very own mom and dad. Pro Tip: This whole setting-a-good-example thing will really come in handy when the kids are drafting up those fear-inducing rehearsal dinner speeches one day.

Sixth: Commit Rather Than Getting Committed

Commit to the LORD whatever you do, and he will establish your plans. (Proverbs 16:3)

This is a topic I feel we need to chat about, as I so wish somebody had taken the time to discuss it with me.

I grew up a good little God/Daddy-fearing Southern girl, who outside of the occasional Fuzzy Navel (aka a beverage available at your local gas station, rocking out with next-to-nothing-percent alcohol content), I was a gold-star sober-ita. Even in my college days, I managed to steer clear of concoctions, apart from nursing one light beverage in a red Solo cup all night long at the occasional baseball game afterparty.

Then I had kids. And some of my more-seasoned mom-tribe peeps introduced me to the "five o'clock somewhere" mantra that I never even knew existed.

Which leads me to a series of confessions.

Confession 1: I do a regular girls' night out with my friends.

Confession 2: My husband and I enjoy a glass of wine from our bar cart,

Confession 3: With screaming toddlers in the background, bills stacking up, and laundry that isn't gonna fold itself, it's so easy to think *Mommy needs a glass of wine.*

Confession 4: I'd much rather be dependent on my God than on my next glass of Rosé.

Have you ever found yourself having similar feelings? I started thinking about this whole "mommy juice" phenomenon, and I grew uncomfortable with the accessory of it all. I would be absolutely devastated if I began allowing myself, and especially my children, to believe that this whole "coffee till cocktail hour" lifestyle was required for managing the role of mom, because, if truth be told, my kids are what make me *want* to get up in the morning—and not just because they are screaming into the monitor at 6:00 a.m. that their sock just fell off. The smiles on my girls' faces are what remind me that love lives here. And their hugs, well, let's just say it isn't a good day till we've laid on the floor snuggling for hours on end.

So it got me thinking: Are our children getting the *best* of us or the *rest* of us?

On some days, our best will be rock-star level. On other days (a lot of the days), our best really will be just the rest of whatever we have to offer after shuffling through another day of #MomLife.

I want my children to have the best, so I will give them my best. *Not* my perfect, but my best. I'd wager that you agree. Even on the days when our tanks have been sitting on empty for quite some time, we can commit them to Christ, and He will provide us with that divine drive that no antidepressant, yoga class, or cocktail ever could (Colossians 3:23).

It's not going to be rainbows and sunshine every day. But this life is truly a gift, friend. This journey of motherhood is a crazy, beautiful ride.

So I feel you, friend. But we are never gonna fill our cups if we keep pouring in cocktails or anything else that helps us get through our day. Our cups will only be full if we fill them with Christ. So from now on: "Cheers" to giving our *best* more often than our *rest*.

Seventh: Add One More Label to Your Momma Resume: Head of Heaven Herding

> "Therefore go and make disciples of all nations, baptizing them in the name of the Father and of the Son and of the Holy Spirit, and teaching them to obey everything I have commanded you. And surely I am with you always, to the very end of the age." (Matthew 28:19–20)

I bet you didn't know you were a cow herder? Wait, of course, you did. But have you considered the fact that the single most important thing we can do for our babies is point them to Christ? This means sitting down and sharing the gospel, modeling it as purely as we can, cultivating an environment in which God can call them to Him in His timing, and providing them a pathway to follow Him first.

If, like me, you find yourself fumbling over your words when it comes to the big convos, I leave you with the verse I always point my babies to when they come with the really big questions: "If you declare with your mouth, 'Jesus is Lord,' and believe in your heart that God raised him from the dead, you will be saved" (Romans 10:9).

And as we've chatted about during our entire time together, remember to always cling to our new mommy mantra: *I may not know everything about parenting, but I know the One who does.*

27

Chugga Chugga Choo Choo: Step Right Up to the Grace Train!

Since we just chatted about the challenging world of parenting, I thought we should look at yet another cautionary tale. Friends, last week my girls and I took our weekly trek to the local Chick-fil-A. Business was good because the lines were long and the "It's my pleasures" were flowing faster than salutations at a bustling Southern mall.

The people were nice, and the smells were heavenly. I could almost taste the Polynesian-sauce-laced chicken swirling on my taste buds until a tiny terror rocked the once-peaceful establishment with a bomb-went-off-type disruption.

I looked in horror as a child, probably three years of age, lay prostrate on the floor, kicking his legs and thrashing as if he was enduring a medical episode. He screamed at the top of his small yet boisterous lungs without a care in the world. It became quite clear to us onlookers that this was *not* Junior's first time starring in a production of *Terrible Toddler: The Musical*. We all just stared at this kid like we were viewing a car accident and couldn't look away. Honestly, I started having uncomfortable flashbacks to all the times I've been the momma of the irritable tot who needed to have a quick chat.

I assumed a harried mother would soon swoop in and end this unnecessary disruption, or at least a Child Protective Services worker in the crowd would step up to the plate. But, to my chagrin, this little tantrum lasted for what felt like hours.

Eventually, other patrons began inquiring about the whereabouts of the child's parents. Soon they discovered a disheveled mom seated at a table adjacent to the toddler tizzy. Once approached, we couldn't help but notice the tears streaming down her face and the obvious signs of sleepless nights. This woman was crying out for help almost as much as her little boy—and it broke my momma heart.

There were customers pointing, staring, and exerting intense judgment on this little boy, while all I could think was, *What if it was* your *kid, people!? How would you feel if people were judging you for his behavior?* Side Note: In the future, I feel like in an effort to pro-actively avert these moments of righteous condemnation, on those days when the train just isn't chugging along right, maybe we should don sandwich boards that read "Hi! My threeanger is going through a delightful moment in her developmental schedule. It's called tan-trums. Ask me about all this fun today!" Or, better yet, we could all do each other a solid and quit staring, keep it moving, and maybe even say a little prayer for said momma.

Full Disclosure: Long before I had babies (especially during those awkward high school years), I most definitely was one of those snarky adolescents lurking in the corner, scowling at any child who even dared make a peep in public. Cue all the "Ha! Sucker!" tears as I scream, "Clean up on aisle seven," charge all the iPads like it's my nightly religion, and hold myself back from throwing a chair through a window after my threenager's latest sass session. While I was ignorant to the whole concept of parenting at the time, there was still no excuse for such judgy-wudgy behavior, and I'm thankful God changed my heart the second I heard that first little heartbeat.

As a momma, I totally get it now. This time, in Chick-fil-A, I was in possession of real-life experience and a backpack full of momma empathy. So, I embraced this momma and began to tear up with her. Parenting is tough. As we've learned so many times before, it is not for the faint of heart. The last thing we need is judgment from others. Judgment in our darkest hours, when there doesn't seem to be any escape.

I don't know that momma's story. I don't know what she and her son are experiencing right now, and I don't have to.

Things are not always as they seem.

That momma struggling to keep her children corralled in the grocery-store line may be going through a divorce. That friend who constantly posts the most perfect Instagram photos may be secretly crying out for someone to save her from her hamster-wheel life of pursuing perfection. That mom who constantly shows up late to pick her kid up in carpool line may be working three jobs to provide for him. And, oh yeah, when *your* kids act like raging looneys, their behavior does not mean that *you* aren't getting it right either.

Even though we spend hours and hours teaching our little ones how to behave, there is no guarantee that what we say will affect the actions that come out. I feel you, mommas. And I see you. I see you sitting there, pulling your hair out. I see you crying out to God, begging Him for answers. I can only imagine the frustration that you, too, are experiencing when the little ones take a turn for Terror Town.

Parenting—true, training-focused parenting—is a marathon requiring us to put our noses to the grind and sip on that Gatorade all the way to the finish line. It means late nights. Frustrating but necessary deep discussions. It means sacrifices and occasional struggles. It means curling up in a fetal position at times while screaming out for divine intervention. It means putting everything aside to focus on our top priorities. It is our most difficult role but our most entrusted responsibility. Most importantly, it means *never giving up*.

Rest assured that no matter how hard we work and no matter how much we pour into our children, what comes out is totally up to them. So take a deep breath and relax. We aren't expected to be the puppet masters of our kids' lives. We *are* expected to train them up as they should go, and when they grow old, they will not depart from it (Proverbs 22:6). At least, that's what my Bible says.

I wrote this chapter to remind myself that I have got to be the conductor of my own train, all the while allowing God to direct me on those tracks. I also wrote this to remind us to give grace to all mommas, no matter the situation. "In this world, we are constantly stacked against one another, but at the cross, we stand alongside one another each desperately in need of grace, which is freely given in Christ."[25] We have no clue what is going on in someone else's home. Our mission is never to judge but rather to give a whole lot of grace and understanding.

So today I encourage you, as my friend and fellow momma warrior, to keep driving your train. Train 'em up! Chugga chugga choo choo! But, remember to give yourself, your precious babies, and all the other families in this world a big dose of God's grace, because His grace is the best gift you can give your children—and your fellow patrons in the Chick-fil-A line too.

28

Handprints on Their Hearts

So many people refer to mommas as warriors, and I've occasionally scoffed at that because it seems so, well, *dramatic*. But the Bible confirms our designation as such: "Like arrows in the hands of a warrior are children born in one's youth" (Psalm 127:4).

When I think of a warrior and her arrows, I get a very detailed image of this warrior sharpening her arrows, tending to them, and polishing them. She is trained to make her arrows precise and prepped for landing with intention. Then, at some point, it comes time for her to launch her arrows into the world.

What a cool metaphor for what we moms do every day.

Out of all the things we have learned about together, I hope you cling to this one verse: "He must become greater; I must become less" (John 3:30.). Our most important job in motherhood is not to convince our children to crave broccoli. But rather to crave Christ. "Seeking to raise a child who loves the Lord with all his heart, soul and mind, is our highest calling as parents."[26] We can't force them to engage in an intimate relationship with Christ devoid of sin, but we can model for them an imperfect human striving day in and day out to be more like Him.

- So teach your kids to count … *their blessings.*
- Show them how to walk … *with Christ.*

- Counsel them on how to do ... *what is right.*
- And love on them ... *with everything you have.*

Parenting is the perfect combination of *Mr. Toad's Wild Ride* and the receipt of a golden ticket that would make even Willy Wonka jealous. There are highs and lows, insides and outs, but the one thing that stands the test of all the seasons is that God has entrusted these little earthly embodiments of His love and provision to our care. This whole journey is not about us, not even about our kids. It's about *Him* and what we do for Him here on this earth.

"Our children don't need us to be the perfection of Christ. They need to see us in pursuit of Christ. They need us to point them to Christ."[27] Are we pushing our children to be the best, or are we pushing them toward the arms of the Christ?

God isn't concerned about how many trophies or attaboys our children have earned, but rather what they have done for His kingdom. Instead of looking at our parenting as a game to be figured out or an award to seek, let's look at how we can use this privilege to honor Him. Even though life gets busy at times, motherhood is an aspect of our souls that never gets pushed to the wayside and never loses its significance.

Our most important job in motherhood is not to convince our children to crave broccoli. But rather to crave Christ.

It often occurs to me that my role as a parent is much more significant than a chauffeur or PTO attender or babysitter or bath giver or boo-boo kisser or personal chef. My greatest role, as a parent, is to impart the teachings and promises of God by leaving daily handprints on my children's hearts.

Life moves at such a stressfully rapid pace. It seems as if we are lying on the birthing table one minute and standing at graduation the next. I want to soak up every moment and ensure that I am pouring into my babies the love and promises that God provides. But heaven knows I'm forgetful. And scattered. And overwhelmed. And at times, if I'm brutally honest, ill-equipped for this awesome responsibility. One of the biggest struggles I face as a momma is the fear that I won't get it right. That I won't do all the things and impart all the wisdom. It's overwhelming—and *scary*.

So I recently sat down one afternoon and penned an open letter to my babies. A checklist of sorts containing all the things I want them to know. All the little tidbits of wisdom I wish to impart that I pray don't get lost in the daily grind. I won't bore you with the whole letter (if you want the whole letter, I'll put it up on my website for you), but thought I would share some of the handprints I am praying to leave on my girls' hearts, in hopes that maybe they inspire you as well.

My prayer is that if you, too, are a busy momma, this list might help you on days when you can't get your shoes tied correctly, much less win the award for Wisdom Imparter of the Year. Cut these out, grab a glue stick, smack 'em in those baby books, and breathe. You've got this, momma. Through Christ who gives you strength.

- You are so loved—Ephesians 3:16–21; 1 John 4:16
- You are a gift from God—Psalm 127:3
- You are enough *in Christ*—Ephesians 1:6
- You are prayed for—Ephesians 1:18
- You are beautiful just as God designed you—Song of Songs 4:7
- Your inner beauty is more important than your outer beauty—1 Samuel 16:7
- Your life has meaning and purpose—Jeremiah 29:11
- You can achieve anything you dream—Proverbs 16:3; Psalm 37:4
- You should give your best in everything you do—Colossians 3:23
- You will fail at times and that's okay—2 Corinthians 12:9–10

- Your heart should be filled with happiness and thankfulness—Psalm 126:3
- You have nothing to fear—Deuteronomy 31:6
- Your kindness is never a weakness—Ephesians 4:32
- You are not alone—Psalm 46:1
- You will find everything you ever need in Christ—Philippians 4:6–7
- You are a light in this world—Matthew 5:16

CHEERS TO ...

- Seeking Christ's face like it's your job.
- Knowing that when it's all said and done, you can do these seven things to honor Christ in your parenting: pre-prayering yourself and your kiddos, being thankful, giving grace, blessing those broken roads, being a good monkey, committing yourself to giving your best, and herding those cows.
- Helping a sister out. Judging other parenting styles is for the birds.
- Embracing one another, and maybe even learning from one another. It's a much better use of your time! Chugga chugga choo choo!
- Today's Celebration: Cut out the list of scriptural affirmations, make copies if you need to do so, and place one in each of your children's baby books. Or write them a personal letter and enclose those Scriptures to be gifted to them at a birthday later in life. Maybe even consider taping one to your bathroom mirror to remind yourself of all God's promises to *you* as well.

Take a few minutes today and intentionally affirm your children. Tell them you love them. Tell them you are proud of them. Consider starting a new tradition at bedtime, or even once or twice a week if bedtimes are hairy-scary, where the entire family sits down to read a book (bonus points if it's a devotional of some kind). Spend that time being intentional about pouring God's Word into your children. Remind yourself that you are only responsible for what is poured in. God will take care of what comes out!

PART X

This Too Shall Pass (Boogers and Poopy Diapers Included)

Mom Confession: I miss going out to eat, and girls' nights, and the ability to hear my own thoughts.

CHEERS TO ...

Truth #10 – You Will Get Through This

Every day will not be great, but there will be something great about every day. The seasons of life come and go, and if we look for it, there is something to celebrate in each one.

....

To every thing there is a season,
and a time to every purpose under heaven.

ECCLESIASTES 3:1 KJV

29

The Tale of the Next Best Thing

Take delight in the LORD,
and he will give you the desires of your heart.

PSALM 37:4

As I am writing to you, it is snowing in Birmingham, Alabama. ALABAMA, people. I did not say Upstate New York. I repeat, *Alabama.* The snow is truly beautiful, and I know that after a few days it will be gone, but all I can think is, *Hurry up and get out of here, snow! I'm ready for the beach!* Seasonal restlessness is so real. It creeps up on us when we least expect it, and I'm not just talking about when the snow melts.

When I was fifteen, all I wanted was the freedom that came with getting my driver's license—also known as my "Freedom for Us All" phase.

In my first semester of college, all I wanted was to get married, have all the babies, and build the perfect house tucked behind the beautiful white picket fence—now lovingly referred to as my "Get a Grip, You Naive Little Southern Girl" phase.

When my babies were newborns, all I wanted was for them to crawl and hug me back, so we could bond like the inseparable partners I had destined us to be pre-conception—also known as my "Overzealous Pass the Chill Pill" phase.

And when my babies grew into lively toddlers, all I wanted was a five-minute period of silence, in a spa, with a free masseuse attending to my rode-hard-and-put-up-wet, frazzled existence—referred to now as my "Jesus, Be an Escape Door" phase.

Do you find yourself in any of those phases? Always striving for that next step rather than soaking up the one you're in? I have noticed that those seasonal-restlessness moments tend to creep back up often during motherhood.

For example, when my little girls were confined to bouncy seats and play yards, I constantly thought, *Oh, how great it will be when they can roam and walk on their own.* When they finally *did* find their "movement," I thought, *Oh, how great preschool will be when they are structured rather than terrorizing all the villages.* And let's not forget the majesty we mistakenly thought we had achieved after potty training, until we were met with the daunting chore of chasing around a naked-bottomed toddler who swore off underwear for good.

The seasonal restlessness *really* struck when my Google searches went from "where can I find the best sangria in town?" to "who sells the comfiest pajama pants?" It's funny how my childhood punishments of going to bed early, napping, and not leaving my house have become my adult #LifeGoals.

With each phase, we realize how great we had it just a few days before the "new season" arrived, don't we? One minute we are rocking the cuddliest baby in the world, and then we pull out our phone to do our shame-inducing Facebook scroll only to discover that half our friends are out partying like it's 1999.

We often find ourselves striving for the next step. Next week. Next season. It always seems like the *next* season will be easier. Life is funny like that. It makes us see through rose-colored glasses when we look at certain things.

When my kids were infants, I admit I would often feel like I was missing out on big nights like New Year's Eve, when I felt like every single person in the world was out noshing on delectable cuisine and dancing into the wee hours of the morning. All the while, yours truly was smudging spit up into my three-day-old T-shirt in a soiled glider trapped in the confines of #MomLife. I felt gross, and straight up ready for the next chapter.

Fast forward to this year, when I danced like a fool and sang with my two new pint-sized besties. Our late-night jam session/dance party fulfilled me in a way that no champagne toast could ever equal because God had given me the contentment that only *He* can provide. As glamorous as that evening certainly was *not*, I went to sleep at a normal hour, didn't overspend on inflated holiday dining prices, and woke up the next day ready to dominate this thing called life.

The truth is, there are challenges in every season of parenting. There are challenges in every season of *life*. If we just accept that fact, it will allow us to appreciate *today* infinitely more. If we could only look around us and soak in our *current* moment, we would find a place of peace and solace there that doesn't exist anywhere else.

When we search for our "happy" in the here and now—the kids we are raising, the friends we have, or the husband we are married to—we are going to come up empty every single time because those humans will disappoint us. And throw up on us. And beckon us at 3:00 a.m. to wipe their snotty noses. But *God* never disappoints, and He is in the business of being all we need. Searching for contentment in Him, rather than in the season we are in or in the people we love, will always yield us levels of joy we could never find anywhere else.

When people ask me what my favorite verse is, I never hesitate to state confidently, Proverbs 15:13: "A happy heart makes the face cheerful." This has become my fight song, if you will. It is my reminder that what I put in my heart, will come out to share with others. Lord have mercy, do my children make me happy, but God's goodness and grace and mercy, now *they* are a shot of happiness that nothing on this earth and no season you can ever experience will ever provide.

"When we repurpose our passions to fit the season of life we're in, amazing things happen. Joy happens. Growth happens. We're invited to watch as God takes what we offer Him and uses it for the Kingdom. After all, God's purposes and passion for His people are always in season."[28]

If you still need some help in this area, might I suggest a few "fixes" my hubby and I have discovered. If you find yourself lusting after another stage in your life, adjust your current one to meet those needs. For example, I love to have date night, but I *don't* like paying babysitters. So one night a week, we tuck our kids in a little early, my husband picks up my favorite takeout meal, and we sit at the dining room table. I light candles. We might even throw on some cool jazz in the background. *Fancy, huh?* Not so much. It's called survival. But it's making the best of what we've got these days. And if I'm being honest, my pants fit better and my wallet doesn't seem as light.

You have been given *today* in all its glory. So enjoy it. Live it up! And remember that even though you may be discouraged by the daily grind, soak up all the little moments because what will seem like small, insignificant moments now will be much larger, memorable ones down the road.

Now when I read Ecclesiastes 3:1 KJV, I see it more like this: "To every thing there is a season, and a time for every purpose under heaven [spaghetti stains and poopy diapers included]." Thank the good Lord for seasons.

30

These Are the Days ...

How many times have you found yourself strolling through the grocery store (more like racing feverishly while bribing your kids with cookies and balloons until you can finally reach the checkout line) when all of a sudden, a sweet older woman approaches you and says, "My, aren't they precious! Soak it up, sweetie. They'll be gone and out of your house before you even realize it!"

Well, I was standing in the checkout line the other day with my little ones when a sweet old lady (Side Note: Her name was Rosemary—cue all the precious-old-lady feels!) approached me and complimented my girls' behavior! Like, hold up for a minute! Can I get an award for this or something? But seriously, for a moment, I thought, *Oh lady, travel home in the car with us for about ten minutes and see if your sweet words last.* Disclaimer: I was also recovering from having *just* chastised the littlest one for screaming, "Look at that woman's BIG BOOTY!" as loud as she possibly could, moments prior to this interaction, so Rosemary's kindness appeared to me almost as a hallucination. Come to think of it, maybe it *was* a hallucination.

Then Rosemary's aged eyes peered deep into my soul, and she delivered that fateful one liner: "Soak this in, doll. One day you'll wish you were right back here in this checkout line, doing it all over again. These are the days."

Yeah, I'm gonna go with probably *not*, Rosemary.

I swear those unassuming little ladies who compliment random children and comment on the beauty of life have got to be angels sent directly from God to remind us of all things for which we have to be grateful.

But how many of those times did we secretly want to punch grandma in the face just a little bit? Because we are in the thick of it, sisters, and the whole "the days are long, but the years are short" mentality is rage-inducing right now. Let a woman live, for God's sake! Let me love my kids but also want to lock them in their rooms to hide and eat candy in my bathroom. Let me secretly cry in the dressing room at Target because my kid threw a tantrum *yet again*, even though we've been over good behavior 167,832,849 times. And *also*, let me pine away for an escape to Barbados sans kids for about two weeks and not feel guilty about that little dream vacay!

I imagine, as the years pass by, all the barfing incidents, terrible twos, and nightmarish sleep-training memories tend to fade, and we are left with all the cute and cuddly ones. For example, Rosemary most likely does *not* lose sleep over whether her children will wake up the next morning and eat something other than three bites of bread and some juice. Man, am I excited for those days!

But I feel like we'd be really shortchanging ourselves if we couldn't come up with a way to feel the same joy about *today*.

After I laid the kids down for naps that day (rather, laid down treats as if I was alluring Hansel and Gretel to their doom, then gently closed the doors behind them), I got to thinking. Maybe Rosemary had been sent by God to shake me out of my momma funk and remind me of how much I really *do* have to be grateful for. Maybe she was sent to take the edge off a clearly tired and stressed out momma. *Or maybe* she was meant to remind me of this simple truth:

These *are* the days.

There is no day like this one.

Today will never come again.

Rather than wishing for tomorrow, or for that dream sans-kids Barbados getaway, we can embrace today with a renewed vigor of hope and gratitude. Because maybe one day we *will* take that trip, and buy those shoes, and check all the things off the good ole bucket list. There actually *will* be days that we miss the spaghetti stains and the burp cloths. There *will* come a day when we long to hear a baby crying down the hallway, rather than praying our phones will ring with the sound of our adult child on the other end.

In fact, as an example, I was rocking my littlest one to sleep this weekend, when out-of-the-blue stressful thoughts began savagely invading my somewhat peaceful brain: *What about those dishes, Erin? You forgot to clean the kitchen table after lunch! When are you gonna take that beach trip, sport all the cool new fashions, and walk along the shoreline with your favorite margarita in hand, ya loser?! And guess what homegirl from back home is doing tonight? Yep. Justin Timberlake concert in Hotlanta. You know you want to bring sexy back too, girl.*

Just as I felt my blood pressure rising with all these thoughts swirling around in my head, my little girl's hand gently stroked my arm. She had no clue that her simple gesture soothed her overstressed and FOMO'd ("fear of missing out" for all you awesomely not-all-the-way-hip-with-the-lingo mommas—who are still the coolest, by the way) out momma instantly.

Today I am rocking my little girl comfortably in our glider tucked away from the craziness of the real world. But one day I'll be rocking nervously back and forth in my bed, waiting to see the headlights from her car pour onto my comforter, signaling she has made it home safely once again.

Today I am folding her blankets and towels only to discover her playing Hide and Seek tucked deep in the laundry basket among all the dryer sheets and warmth. But one day I'll be reluctantly walking the aisles of Target with her, shopping for dorm linens, shower shoes, and bath caddies.

Today I am reading her bedtime stories and singing soft little tunes as I have the privilege of tucking her into bed. But one day I'll be reading her name on a graduation pamphlet and fighting back tears as I sing hymns of congratulatory praise for all her accomplishments.

Today I am cutting the edges off my toddler's toast to make sure she enjoys every bite. But one day I'll be desperately trying to avoid cutting the helicopter mommy cord on her wedding day, wishing more than anything to be "slaving away" on the heart-shaped PB&Js in the kitchen again.

Today I am hoping she doesn't scream "Mommy" one more time, while I hide under the dining room table searching for any amount of sanity that might be miraculously hidden under there. But tomorrow I will be giving any amount of money to hear her say my name each time a need arises in her precious adult life.

So the pining after another season can be finished. The laundry, the dishes, and the tidying can take a seat. I'll get around to it—whenever that may be. Today I'm gonna let my kids be little and soak up every last minute of it. "Whatever season you're in, there's one way to do your season well: embrace it."[29]

Today we have these babies to raise. Nobody said it was going be easy. So let's just do it. It's corny, I know. But let's do it. And let's look for all the awesome reasons we have to be thankful—even if that reason is that one day, way down the road, we will look back and relish those grocery-store moments, as we stand there buying caramels and denture cream, having a "Rosemary" moment of our very own.

Take a look right now at whom and what God has provided you. Because today is the day. This is the day you have been given in this life, in this moment, in this hour.

These really are the days, girl.

> This is the day that the LORD has made;
> Let us rejoice and be glad in it.

PSALM 118:24 ESV

Conclusion

The Thrivin' Tribe: A Love Letter to You

Wow. We did it, friend. We learned that we *don't* have to get it all right, we *don't* have to win Pinterest Princess of the Year, and we *don't* have to feel alone and scared at 2:00 a.m.

We *do* get to love those sweet babies, we *do* get to experience all the snuggles and slobbery kisses, and we *do* get to see the face of Christ through our children's eyes.

I hope you feel heard. I hope you have seen yourself somewhere on the pages of this book, and I pray that you feel community. You are not alone, momma. We are all in this together. There will still be many moments you feel overwhelmed. There will still be early morning crying sessions. And there will still be fears. But you can take heart in the fact that God has designed the answers to all those moments for you. He is the architect of your own little yellow brick road, and He will see you through it all.

In the moments you need an immediate pick me up, cling to these truths:

- When you feel unworthy, remember your worth is in the Lord (Psalm 139:13–15).
- When you feel uncomfortable with something about your appearance, remember God designed you, and you are

perfect just the way you are (Ecclesiastes 3:11; Song of Songs 4:7).

- When you feel weak, remember your strength comes from God. Plus, you have an incredible support system that He has provided for you—in family and friends (Philippians 4:13).
- When you feel scared, know that God has already designed every step of your life plan. He already knows what is planned for you, and He has all the answers to your life questions. All you have to do is call on His name, and He will comfort you with His presence and the promise of a bright future (Jeremiah 29:11).

When you feel overwhelmed, remember that you do not have to go at this life alone. Every day will not be great, but there will be something great about every day. Look for the positives in life and emphasize those. Often something as simple as your frame of mind dictates the way your day plays out (Ecclesiastes 7:14).

Know that *in Christ* you are enough. *You* are beautiful. *You* are strong. *You* are brave. *You* can handle what today has to bring because God is with you every step of the way.

Now I am going to end this book the way I started it, but this time, we are going to say it together. From now on, whenever you feel completely clueless about this whole motherhood journey, cling to the one phrase that will see you through it all. Cheers to the fact that: "We may not know everything about motherhood, but we know the *One* who does."

Cheers to the diaper years!

Cheers to . . . Scripture Resource

This section is meant to serve as a handy-dandy quick reference for all those times you need someone to hold your hand. Look at this whenever you are having all the emotions. I'll be there cheering you on, but, even more importantly, so will Christ.

When you feel **angry**:
    Cheers to the peace you have in Christ.
        Ephesians 4:26–27; 4:31–32
        James 1:19–20

When you feel **impatient**:
    Cheers to the model of patience you have in Christ.
        Hebrews 10:36

When you feel **judgy**:
    Cheers to remembering that you are not responsible for anyone's choices but your own.
        Matthew 7:1–5; 12:34
        Ephesians 4:29
        Philippians 4:8

When you feel a **lack of confidence**:
    Cheers to the confidence you have in Christ.
        Psalm 81:10
        Colossians 3:16
        Hebrews 4:16
        Hebrews 10:35–36

When you feel **lonely**:
>*Cheers to* knowing you are never alone in Christ.
>>Deuteronomy 31:6
>>Isaiah 43:1–5
>>Matthew 28:20
>>Hebrews 13:5

When you feel a **loss of control**:
>*Cheers to* the fact that you never had control in the first place.
>>Psalm 18:2
>>Proverbs 16:9
>>John 16:33

When you feel **mom guilt**:
>*Cheers to* knowing that Christ gives you limitless grace.
>>Isaiah 43:18–19
>>Romans 12:2

When you feel the **pressure** of others:
>*Cheers to* standing firm in your faith and relying on Christ to guide you.
>>Proverbs 4:23
>>Luke 6:45
>>Romans 12:2
>>1 Corinthians 16:14
>>Galatians 1:10

When you feel **tired** and in need of rest:
>*Cheers to* finding exuberance in Him.
>>Psalm 61:2–4
>>Psalm 62:1–2
>>Matthew 11:28
>>Galatians 6:9

When you feel **unattractive**:
>*Cheers to* recognizing the beauty and worth you have in Christ, even on those days when you can't see it yourself. Christ designed you perfectly—just the way you are.

Genesis 1:27
Psalm 139:14
1 Corinthians 6:19–20
2 Corinthians 4:16–20

When you feel **unforgiveable** and need a little (or *a lot of*) grace:

Cheers to worshiping a Savior who died for your sins and took away all your transgressions.

Romans 3:21–26
Romans 5:6–8
Romans 8:1–2
1 Corinthians 1:30
2 Corinthians 5:15, 21
2 Corinthians 9:8
Ephesians 1:1–8
Ephesians 2:4–5

When you feel **unhappy**:

Cheers to the joy you have in Christ.

Psalm 37:4
Psalm 146:5
Habakkuk 3:17–19
Romans 15:13
Philippians 4:4

When you feel **unloved**:

Cheers to the truth that God loves you, *always*, no matter the circumstances.

Romans 5:8
Romans 8:28
Ephesians 3:17–19
1 John 3:1

When you feel **unsure**:

Cheers to the fact that God will always guide your path.

Proverbs 3:5–6

Jeremiah 17:7–8
Jeremiah 29:11
Ephesians 5:1–2
Philippians 4:19
Hebrews 10:35–36

When you feel **unworthy**:
Cheers to discovering your worth in Christ.
Deuteronomy 14:2
Luke 12:7
2 Corinthians 12:9
Galatians 2:16
Philippians 2:13
Hebrews 4:16

When you feel **weak**:
Cheers to finding your strength in Christ.
1 Chronicles 16:11
2 Chronicles 15:7
2 Corinthians 12:9–10
Galatians 6:9
Ephesians 3:20
Philippians 4:19

When you feel **worried** or **scared**:
Cheers to the security you have in Christ.
Joshua 1:9
Psalm 55:22
Proverbs 3:5–6
Isaiah 43:1–4
Matthew 6:25–27; 34
Luke 12:22–28
Philippians 4:6–7
Hebrews 13:6
1 Peter 5:7

Acknowledgments

To my Lord and Savior, I surrender this book to you to do with it as you see fit. Thank you for convicting me to extend my hand to my fellow mommas and gifting me this beautiful message of finding fulfillment in you alone. Every word here came from you, and you are the One who deserves all the praise.

To my babies. You are my world. I wrote this book for three reasons. One, I am so madly in love with this crazy journey of parenting you two that I felt the need to document it for you and whomever else stumbles upon it. My prayer is that this book will encourage and uplift fellow mommas along this beautiful journey. Second, I want you to know that you can do anything imaginable that Christ lays on your heart and that you devote yourself to doing. And finally, I wrote this book to let you know that even during the not-so-awesome moments along the mommyhood journey, it's still the best earthly blessing God designed. Even though you didn't come with little instruction manuals tied to your tiny ankles, you have taught me everything I ever needed to know about being a momma. Your smiles and giggles remind me joy lives here; your hugs and kisses remind me that love abounds here; and your open hearts are the perfect proof that Christ is all we need.

To my parents. I'm not even sure where to begin, but I will state unequivocally that you are the greatest parents the world has ever known. There, I said it. Daddy, you have my permission to rip this page out and have it framed. Mom, I could never dream of a greater cheerleader, accountability partner, nurturer, or example of a loving mother. Thank you for all the things that are so uniquely you. Thank you for selflessly sacrificing every single Thursday for four months so that I could write this love story about motherhood. Daddy, this goes without saying, but I'm the biggest daddy's girl there ever was—and I wear that label with great pride. Thank you for serving as the strongest, most courageous role model I've ever known. My grit and my commitment on this journey of life—well, that's all you, man.

To my husband, Marshall, who paused some sporting event one night back in 2015 so that this small-town girl with big dreams could tell him she had decided to write a book. The crazy part is that you actually believed I could and cheered me on to the finish line. You encouraged me to keep going during the highs, lows, and everything in between, and you threw me my first-ever surprise party right in the middle of my toughest month of writing, just to remind me why it truly is so important to pause and celebrate every season. Cheers, babe.

To my brother, Brad, who became my best friend on August 23, 1988. I would call you my Ride-or-Die Chick here, but to keep it cool, I'll just say this: You're the greatest guy I know. You have supported me from day one and still love me even though I forced you to wear princess dresses until you were twelve years old. Cheers to the sibling years! *Am I right?!* Speaking of siblings, thank you infinitely for marrying Cara. She is the best sister I could have ever dreamed of welcoming into our little fam. Love you both forever!

To my Ninnie. She's looking down in this very moment and most likely getting out her red pen to check my work. *And I couldn't love that more.* To the OG Boss Lady: You took over a trucking company, raised two children alone in your thirties, and still had the time to minister in your church. You worked all day long but still had time to play Pollyanna with me at night. You taught me everything I know about passion, dedication, and the top-three secrets to success: grace, gumption, and a perfectly polished strand of pearls. You said

I'd write one day. I'd like to think you were that secret voice in my ear each morning at 2:00 a.m. whispering, "Keep going, doll baby. Keep going."

To my Mamaw. You are the one who taught me I am special just the way I am. I have never felt so loved, so understood, and so valued than when I am sitting in the rocking chair right beside you. My favorite moments growing up are when we would sit at your kitchen table, eating your famous fried bologna sandwiches with chips and french onion dip while simultaneously solving all the world's problems. It was in those moments, when it wasn't about Pinterest perfection, that I learned it's really all about how you make people feel, the moments you share, and the memories you make together. People call us twins from time to time, and I have never had a greater honor.

To Jayna. You are the unicorn friend I've always been waiting to find. We locked eyes in the lobby of our kids' ballet class back in 2016, and it's been a dream friendship since day one. By the way, that Ride-or-Die Chick section … that's all you, girl. Love you forever, bestie.

To my tribe. My word for 2017 was *friendship*, and boy did God show up. He welcomed friends into my life that feel much more like long-lost sisters. I love you all dearly and couldn't do this life without you. I gotta say, our Hot Mess Express is the greatest one of all time. I am going to list you by name because I want each and every one of you to know how much you mean to me. Here goes: Jayna. Misty. Shelley. Carrie. Candice. Haley. Tracy. Bobbie. Jillian. Sarah. Ali. Lauren M. Lindsey. Katie. Patti. Kelly. Erin. Julie. Caroline. Suzanne. Leighton. Marilyn. Calley. Aunt Kaye. Mrs. Betsy. Mrs. Cindy. Mrs. Rita. Mrs. Kathy. Mrs. Deb. Mrs. Carolyn. You ladies make this phrase real in my life: "Strong Women. We *are* them. We *know* them. We are *raising* them."

To Julie Gwinn. I chose not to type "to my agent" because you are *so* much more than that. You are my mentor, my confidant, and my friend. You met a mom with a notebook full of ideas in February of 2016 and chose to take a chance on her. That chance has turned into the most beautiful friendship and avenue for receiving God's blessings. Thank you for choosing me. In this field, it only takes one person to give you a chance, and you are my person. Looking forward to continuing to do big things with you as my co-pilot.

To Carlton Garborg, David Sluka, Michelle Winger, Jeanna Harder, Nina Derek, Bill Watkins, Tonia Kuter, Sarah Peterson, Christy Distler, and all my BroadStreet Publishing family. I say *family* because that is what we have become. We started off as parties interested in creating a book for moms who needed hope and maybe a little laughter to thrive during those rough parenting days. But our team quickly realized that we are on a mission to revolutionize the mommy mind-set and energize women with the hope of discovering fulfillment in Christ alone. I will never be able to thank you adequately for taking a chance on me. I am indebted to you for your diligence, and your commitment to this message and to me as an author. That reminds me, I need to send up another round of cookies soon.

To you, my newest bestie. Thank you so much for taking a chance on this book with a catchy title and an adorable baby on the cover. I hope you feel loved, because you are, *dearly*. I would love to get to know you better and invite you to hit me up at my little corner of the internet any time. My door and email inbox (erinbrownhollis@gmail.com) are always open—*especially around that fun 2:00 a.m. wake-up call these days*. Always remember: You have been chosen, you are strong, you are never alone, and you will always be enough in Christ! Cheers to the diaper years, my friend!

Notes

1 Heidi St. John, *Becoming Mom Strong: How to Fight with All That's in You for Your Family and Your Faith* (Carol Stream, Illinois: Tyndale Momentum, 2017), 248.

2 Maggie Combs, *Unsupermommy: Release Expectations, Embrace Imperfection, and Connect to God's Superpower* (Racine, Wisconsin: BroadStreet Publishing Group, LLC, 2017), 105.

3 Jeannie Cunnion, *Mom Set Free: Find Relief from the Pressure to Get It All Right* (New York: Howard Books, 2017), 114.

4 Lara Casey, *Cultivate: A Grace-Filled Guide to Growing an Intentional Life* (Nashville: W Publishing, 2017), 104.

5 Jill Savage, *No More Perfect Moms: Learn to Love Your Real Life* (Chicago: Moody Publishers, 2013), 36.

6 Cunnion, *Mom Set Free*, 88.

7 Ibid., 78.

8 Savage, *No More Perfect Moms*, 37.

9 Casey, *Cultivate*, 188.

10 Priscilla Shirer, *Fervent: A Woman's Battle Plan for Serious, Specific and Strategic Prayer* (Nashville, B & H Publishing Group, 2015), 141.

11 St. John, *Becoming Mom Strong*, 50.

12 Casey, *Cultivate*, 169.

13 Ibid., 170.

14 Ibid., 63.

15 Cunnion, *Mom Set Free*, 15.

16 Casey, *Cultivate*, 219.

17 Savage, *No More Perfect Moms*, 34.

18 St. John, *Becoming Mom Strong*, 140–41.

19 The following list is based on another "Checklist for Encouragers" found in the NIV Life Application Study Bible (Grand Rapids: Zondervan; Carol Stream: Tyndale House, 2011), 2019.

20 Emily Ley, *Grace Not Perfection: Embracing Simplicity, Celebrating Joy* (Nashville: Thomas Nelson, 2016), 9.

21 Cunnion, *Mom Set Free*, 115.

22 Ibid., 22.

23 St. John, *Becoming Mom Strong*, 25.

24 Ibid.

25 Cunnion, *Mom Set Free*, 115–16.

26 Ibid., 63.

27 Ibid., 17.

28 St. John, *Becoming Mom Strong*, 80.

29 Casey, *Cultivate*, 52.

Connect with Erin

Erin Brown Hollis is a proud Bama girl, writer, speaker, lawyer, friend, lunchbox packer, boo-boo kisser, sweatpants-wearing momma to her two precious girls: Bellalise (age five), a sweet, gentle-natured soul, and Annalise (age four going on fourteen), the life of every party. She met her husband, Marshall, during law school and dragged that Cajun boy back to the Heart of Dixie, a place he now proudly calls home as well. They live in Birmingham, where their dining room is currently being used for laundry overflow. Outside of writing, Erin's hobbies include scrapbooking, tennis, traveling, *Friends* marathons, crafting, cooking with her girls, and a clean fridge—an outright miracle worth celebrating these days.

When she isn't attending toddler tea parties or wiping up spaghetti stains, you can find Erin writing on her blog: ErinBrownHollis. com and on Facebook/Instagram/Twitter/Pinterest @erinbrownhollis. She welcomes all moms to find a community of love and acceptance on her site, where she shares recipes, crafts, and encouragement weekly. She believes that all moms, no matter their story, are amazing, and loves to see them pursuing their passions, whether that be in a Mommy-and-Me-Zumba class or the center of the boardroom in a pair of killer stilettos. Lastly, and probably most importantly, she believes in making every day a celebration—so if you haven't found a reason to celebrate yet today, tell 'em Erin told you to live it up, girl! *Cheers!*